Transforming Insights from
Respected Husbands & Wives

The Best Advice
I Ever Got on

Marriage

Compiled by **Jim Daly**

PRESIDENT & CEO OF **FOCUS ON THE FAMILY**

WORTHY
PUBLISHING

FOCUS
ON THE FAMILY

A Focus on the Family book published by
Worthy Publishing, a division of Worthy Media, Inc., 134 Franklin Road, Suite 200, Brentwood,
Tennessee 37027

HELPING PEOPLE EXPERIENCE THE HEART OF GOD

Focus on the Family and the accompanying logo and design are federally registered trademarks
of Focus on the Family, Colorado Springs, CO 80995.

eBook available at www.worthypublishing.com

Audio distributed through Oasis Audio; visit www.oasisaudio.com

Library of Congress Control Number: 2012941811

All Scripture quotations, unless otherwise indicated, are taken from the *Holy Bible, New International Version*®, *NIV*®. Copyright © 1973, 1978, 1984 by Biblica, Inc.™ Used by permission of Zondervan. All rights reserved worldwide (www.zondervan.com).

Scripture quotations marked AMP are from *The Amplified Bible*, copyright © 1954, 1958, 1962, 1964, 1965, 1987 by The Lockman Foundation. Used by permission.

Scripture quotations marked ESV are from The Holy Bible, English Standard Version®, copyright © 2001 by Crossway Bibles, a publishing ministry of Good News Publishers. Used by permission. All rights reserved.

Scripture quotations marked NKJV are from the New King James Version. Copyright © 1982 by Thomas Nelson, Inc. Used by permission. All rights reserved.

Scripture quotations marked NLT are from the Holy Bible, *New Living Translation*, copyright © 1996 by Tyndale House Foundation. Used by permission of Tyndale House Publishers, Inc., Carol Stream, Illinois 60188. All rights reserved.

"Make Love a Verb" is taken from *Staying in Love Participant's Guide* by Andy Stanley. Copyright © 2010 by North Point Ministries, Inc.. Used by permission of Zondervan. www.zondervan.com

"Putting Sex on the Calendar" by Jill Savage is adapted from an article originally published in *Marriage Partnership*, a publication of Christianity Today, International, Summer 2005.

For foreign and subsidiary rights, contact Riggins International Rights Services, Inc.; www.rigginsrights.com

ISBN: 978-1-936034-49-9 (hardcover w/ jacket)

Editor: Marianne Hering
Cover Design: Christopher Tobias
Cover Art: © Eric Thomas

Printed in the United States of America

12 13 14 15 16 17 RRD 8 7 6 5 4 3 2 1

CONTENTS

INTRODUCTION:
THE OPEN-HEARTED MARRIAGE

Dr. Greg Smalley

The greatest marriage advice I've ever heard came from one of the most unlikely places: *Dr. Quinn, Medicine Woman.* Remember the CBS television show back in the 1990s about a female doctor in the Old West played by actress Jane Seymour? Once the show ended, Seymour developed a jewelry line with Kay Jewelers called the Open Hearts collection. The fascinating part is the slogan—which I think is the best advice ever for cultivating a thriving marriage: "If your heart is open, love will always find its way in."

Just as Dr. Quinn understood, an open heart is the fundamental prerequisite for a great marriage. Yet many of us struggle to keep our hearts open because openness can feel risky and dangerous. Marriage specialists Arch Hart and Sharon Hart Morris put it this way:

> When a husband and wife love each other, they literally give their hearts to each other for safekeeping. This is such a delicate, trusting act that

any violation or injury of this trust can cause the most painful of reactions.

Imagine taking the very essence of your being—your heart—and placing it in the hands of your spouse. Your heart becomes your mate's to care for, safeguard, cherish, and love. Placing your heart in the hands of another is a giant step of faith. Afterward, you can only wait to see what your spouse will do with your heart. Your desire, of course, is that your spouse will be a safe haven for your heart. And that is your spouse's longing as well.[1]

In your quest to have a thriving marriage, I want to encourage you to make your marriage the safest place possible for your spouse.

Why should this be a top priority? Because to get what you want in your marriage—fun, passion, friendship, love, respect, intimacy, deep connection—each heart must be open to the other. This is the meaning behind the slogan "Open your heart and love will always find its way in." Love will always find its way in because God's love is everywhere (Psalm 119:64). And God's love will flow through your heart to your spouse's when both are open. But a heart will only open up when the relationship feels safe. Therefore, make it your goal to create a marriage that feels like the safest place on earth.

THE SAFEST PLACE ON EARTH

The only way you can intertwine two hearts and become one is when both of you feel emotionally safe. The good news is that you can create a safe atmosphere in your marriage that will allow and encourage both people to open their hearts. But the focus must be on creating *safety*.

Jesus warned against hardening hearts when He commented on divorce: "Moses permitted you to divorce your wives because your hearts were hard" (Matthew 19:8). A closed and hardened heart is the real destroyer of relationships—and therefore something to prevent at all cost. On the other hand, a safe marriage allows both husband and wife to open up and reveal their deepest feelings, thoughts, beliefs, hopes, and dreams. That's true intimacy!

Creating safety isn't a psychobabble phrase. In fact, it's something that our heavenly Father already does for us: "The name of the LORD is a strong tower; the righteous run to it and are safe" (Proverbs 18:10). Isn't it amazing the God of this universe goes out of His way to make us feel safe? He wants our hearts to be open, and hearts open when they feel safe. I want to model my marriage after what God does with me.

So what's the key to creating a marriage that feels like the safest place on earth? The answer is well illustrated by something that happened in my own family.

One morning, we were frantically getting ready to go on a vacation to Disney World. I thought everyone was finally in the car, and every conceivable space was packed with luggage. But then I noticed that Maddy, my middle daughter who was around three at the time, wasn't in her car seat. Instead, she was in the house desperately searching for Gracie, her favorite Beanie Baby. The little yellow praying bunny was her most valuable possession. Maddy never went anywhere without Gracie.

After Maddy located Gracie, she came running out to the car. *Oh no!* I thought, *Maddy is going to lose Gracie, and I don't want to spend all my vacation time traipsing around a mall looking for a replacement!* So as my precious daughter ran toward me, I only had a few seconds to concoct a plan so clever that it would convince Maddy to leave Gracie home.

"Maddy, hold on," I began tentatively. "Actually, Daddy needs you to leave Gracie home."

Maddy blankly stared at me as I continued explaining my brilliant plan. "We need someone to watch the house," I said. "So why don't you put Gracie back in your bed, and she can take care of the house?"

"No!" Maddy shot back. "Barry Wonderful will watch the house. Gracie is coming with us!"

Barry Wonderful? I thought. *Who the heck is Barry Wonderful?*

My wife, Erin, could see my confusion. "You know Barry Wonderful, honey," she said, smiling sarcastically as she explained. "The stuffed Saint Bernard dog you bought Maddy that sings the extremely annoying Barry White songs you thought was so cute!"

"Oh, right," I said. "Sorry about that."

"Maddy, I really need you to leave Gracie home." She gave me a look that said, *Are you crazy? Leave Gracie be-*

hind? This little dance continued for a few seconds as I gave my logical reasons why she should leave the praying bunny at home. Despite my brilliant arguments, Maddy made no move for the house. Finally I got very stern and said, "Go right now and put her back in your bed!"

Maddy, her little head down, tears flowing, made one last attempt. "Is Disney World fun?" she asked.

I instantly changed my strategy and went at the Gracie issue from a new angle. "Disney World is going to be the best vacation we've ever had," I said. "But we have to go now, or we're going to miss our flight! So why don't you put Gracie back on your bed next to Barry Wonderful? Then we can go."

Maddy slowly handed me Gracie. "If Disney World is going to be that fun," she cried, "I love Gracie so much that I want her to go, and I'll watch the house."

Crickets chirped as I silently stood there with my mouth open, trying to comprehend what had just happened. Maddy was actually offering to stay home so Gracie could go on our vacation. I had sudden visions of the movie *Home Alone* where Maddy would be alone fending off burglars.

Suddenly I felt like a total loser. And Erin just sat there shaking her head. So I picked up Maddy, explained that our trip wouldn't be the same without Gracie, and off we went!

Although this story isn't a great example of my stellar parenting skills (this is a marriage book after all!), it's a wonderful illustration of how to create safety.

Watch how emotional safety is built when we do two very important things—the same two things that Maddy did for Gracie.

Creating a marriage that feels like the safest place on earth involves both an *attitude* and an *action*. These two things are actually found in Ephesians 5:29: "For no one ever hated his own flesh, but nourishes and cherishes it, just as Christ does the church" (esv). Cherish and nourish—an attitude and an action. Let's look first at the attitude that we need to have if we are to foster safety in our marriage.

ATTITUDE: RECOGNIZE YOUR MATE'S INCREDIBLE VALUE. CHERISH HIM OR HER.

Recognizing another's value is the heart of *honoring* him or her. By *honoring* your spouse, I mean making the simple decision to place a high value, true worth, and great importance on your spouse by viewing him or her as a priceless gift. This is exactly how Maddy saw Gracie—as someone of enormous value. Maddy cherished Gracie. In the same way honor is a gift we give to our spouse. Honor isn't purchased by one's actions or contingent on emotions. When we honor our spouses, we are giving them distinction whether or not they like it, want it, or deserve it. You just do it; it's a decision you make. The great news is that when you see your spouse as a priceless treasure, your heart will open up to him or her: "For where your treasure is, there your heart will be also" (Luke 12:34). So take a minute right now to list the reasons why your spouse is so valuable. Don't forget to share your list with your spouse.

As wonderful as it is to cherish your spouse because you are aware of his or her incredible worth, this attitude without any action is meaningless: "Let us not love with words or tongue but with actions and in truth" (1 John 3:18). Once you recognize your mate's value, you need to back that attitude with action.

ACTION: SHOW WITH YOUR ACTIONS THAT YOU VALUE YOUR SPOUSE. NOURISH HIM OR HER.

If you want your marriage to feel like the safest place on earth, you must not only pledge to see your mate as valuable, but you must also convey that honor through your words, actions, and deeds.

As Maddy demonstrated by her willingness to give up her trip to Disney World so Gracie could go, *love* really is a verb. Safety is honor in action. Safe people focus on loving the other person rather than measuring how much they are being loved. We need to feed and care for our marriage; we need to nourish it. If you want to know the best way to nourish your spouse, just ask him or her to finish this statement: "I feel loved when you . . ."

At a marriage seminar, I asked over a thousand couples this same question. Listen to some of their answers:

- Pray for me and with me.
- Love and accept me unconditionally.
- Accept my influence; be teachable.

- Allow me to enter your inner world: share your feelings and thoughts.
- Seek to understand me before being understood.
- Validate my feelings.
- Reassure me of your love.
- Act curious about me: ask me lots of questions.
- Spend time with me.
- Plan our future together.
- Serve me in ways that are meaningful to me.
- Have fun and laugh with me.
- Take time to work through conflict.
- Comfort me when I'm down.
- Correct me gently and tenderly.
- Compliment me often.
- Meet my sexual needs.
- Be forgiving when I offend you.
- Tell me how much you appreciate me.
- Lead our family in our spiritual relationship with God.
- Take time to notice what I have done for you and the family.
- Treat me as if God had stamped the words "Handle with Care" on my forehead.

Whatever your spouse's response, keep in mind that these answers offer you a gold mine of information. So be sure to share your answers with your spouse so that you two can work together to make your marriage feel like the safest place on earth. And never forget, "If your heart is open, love will always find its way in."

Someone once asked me if I hosted a dinner party and could invite any famous person or historical figure, who would I invite? I instantly thought about people like Jesus, Abraham Lincoln, Mother Teresa, Moses, C. S. Lewis, Corrie ten Boom, and Billy Graham. Who would you invite?

Now imagine having the opportunity to have dinner with some of the greatest relationship minds of our generation. What questions would you ask?

The great news is that I'm personally inviting you to just such an event. It's as if you've been invited to a special dinner party featuring some of my favorite marriage experts. Bound between the covers of this book is a collection of essays by amazing people that reveal their marriage-transforming advice.

Wherever this book finds you and your spouse, it's my hope the advice within will help you build the marriage you've always dreamed of. One of the common themes that runs through this collection is the importance of open and honest dialogue. I encourage you to read one chapter a week with your spouse. Discuss the ideas that really resonated with you or the thoughts that jumped out in your mind— good or bad. Pray for the Lord's guidance as you read and apply the advice found within these pages.

Together we'll explore the benefits of scheduling sex, the healing power of laughter, and the nine words that pulled one couple's marriage from the brink of disaster. You'll witness how growing as an individual is just as important as growing as a couple.

It's possible not every piece of advice will apply to your current situation. Yet don't forget that circumstances change over time. As you and your spouse journey through the different seasons of your marriage, one of the relationship nuggets found within these pages could very well become vital down the road.

I pray the Lord will bless you in mighty ways as you journey toward a thriving marriage. I'll leave you with one of my favorite quotes on marriage: "A successful marriage requires falling in love many times, always with the same person."[2]

Enjoy falling in love again with your spouse!

July 31, 2012

1. Archibald D. Hart and Sharon Hart Morris, *Safe Haven Marriage: Building a Relationship You Want to Come Home To* (Nashville: Thomas Nelson, 2003), 28.

2. Attributed to journalist Mignon McLaughlin, *Atlantic Monthly*, July 1965.

Dr. Greg Smalley serves as Executive Director of Marriage and Family Formation at Focus on the Family; he is also the author of eleven books. Married nineteen years, Greg and his wife, Erin, live in Colorado with their four children. The Smalleys, who—with help—overcame their own marriage struggles, make a point to study a marriage book together every Christmas.

1

Keep Your Commitment to Your Commitment

Ken Blanchard

In 2012 my wife, Margie, and I will be celebrating our fiftieth wedding anniversary. It's hard to imagine we've been together that long, but as we look back on the years, we see that it has been a wonderful journey of learning. I say *journey of learning* because if you claim your marriage hasn't had any bumps in the road, you probably lie about other things too! Learning to live with someone else and create a loving relationship is a challenge in our society where giving up on marriage seems to be the rule rather than the exception.

FALLING IN LOVE AFTER YOU SAY "I DO"

The challenge of marriage was spelled out clearly several years ago for Margie and me by a young tour guide as he showed us around during our first visit to India. He was in his early twenties and told us that his mom and dad were back home arranging his marriage. Hearing that, I asked him, "Since you have toured with many Americans, what do you think is the main difference between an Indian arranged marriage and a typical American marriage?"

I will never forget his reply. "I think the assumption in an Indian arranged marriage is that over time you will fall in love with the person you marry," said the tour guide. "With American marriages, I get the impression that you fall in love before marriage and then fall out of love during marriage."

The power of the young man's words impacted me so much that I recently shared it when I participated in my nephew's wedding ceremony. I grabbed the hands of the bride and groom and held them as I said, "My hope, my dream, my prayer for you both is that years from now you will look back at your wedding day and realize that it was the day you loved each other the least. May your life together be one of falling in love with each other more every day."

People who were gathered there almost sighed in unison. They knew that it was a wonderful thought—and that it would be a real challenge. Why?

REMEMBER WHY YOU FELL IN LOVE

My observation is that when couples fall in love before they get married, they are focusing on everything positive. You know the old saying "Love is blind." We are usually googly-eyed over each other before we get married. Then, once the marriage vows are said and we start trying to merge our lives together, we begin to recognize little things we didn't notice before. Our attention starts to move from catching each other doing things right to focusing on what might be wrong. Over time, we may forget why we even fell in love if we continue to focus on the negative. If this cycle isn't broken, the journey to divorce court is well on its way.

It is much easier to change a habit or behavior when you are in a supportive, loving environment than when you are continually having your shortcomings highlighted for you.

Margie often says that our marriage really became great when she made the conscious decision to love the total package that was me. That included reexamining the reasons she fell in love with me and realizing that they far outweighed the things about me that bugged her. With that realization came the clarity that it is much easier to change a habit or behavior when you are in a supportive, loving environment than when you are continually having your shortcomings highlighted for you. After all, even though God doesn't make junk, none of us is perfect. We all have things we can work on to make ourselves better partners for life.

DO YOU WANT YOUR
RELATIONSHIP TO WORK?

People ask me all the time if I do marriage counseling. I say, "No, but I'll ask you one question: Do you want your relationship to work? There are only two answers to this question: *Yes* and *no*. If you say, 'Yes, if she (or he) does such and such,' that's really a no answer." The commitment to make a relationship work has to be just that: a commitment.

I'll never forget a time in our relationship when Margie and I hit a rough patch. I was on the faculty at the University of Massachusetts, and she was working on her doctorate in communication studies. Our son, Scott, and daughter, Debbie, were both in elementary school. I was becoming a local hero and being asked to do all kinds of presentations and teaching while Margie had her nose stuck in a book. She felt I wasn't being helpful enough with the kids, and I felt that working on her doctorate wasn't making her a fun person to be around. We were beginning to drift apart. During the height of this period, I was given sabbatical leave with an opportunity to go from Amherst, Massachusetts, to San Diego, California, for a year. I had just been promoted to full professor with tenure, and Margie was about to finish her doctorate. We sat down one night and had a conversation that would make all the difference in our future relationship.

I asked Margie, "Do you want to go to California with me?" What I was really asking was "Do you want to make our relationship work?" Even though these had been rocky times, she said, "Yes, I love you and I want to make our relationship work." My response was also yes. So, with a two-yes commitment, we agreed that we needed help and should seek marriage counseling. We were fortunate to make contact with Maria Bowen, who had been one of Carl Rogers's top graduate students. When we arrived in California, we started meeting with Maria once a week and did so for almost a year.

Marriage counseling doesn't work unless you have two yeses in response to the commitment question. If one or both partners are still trying to decide whether they want to work things out, you can't be honest and open with each other for fear that will be the last straw. But if both individuals are committed to making the relationship work, a good counselor can really help you develop strategies and ways to interact that will build up the relationship rather than tear it down.

Marriage counseling doesn't work unless you have two yeses in response to the commitment question.

IT'S WORTH THE EFFORT

I'll never forget what Peter Drucker, a pioneer in my field of business management, once said: "Nothing good happens by accident." You have to establish a structure for making your marriage work. I love that a lot of young couples today have date nights when, at least twice a month, they get a babysitter and go out together. The rule is that they can't talk about their work or the kids—only about their relationship and how they are doing as a couple. These date nights don't have to be intense or expensive. They can be fun. And what a difference it could make if every married couple scheduled twenty-six date nights a year to focus only on their relationship!

One of the most powerful things Margie and I did while we were going through marriage counseling was to attend a Worldwide Marriage Encounter weekend. This wonderful weekend program, designed for couples, began in the Catholic Church and has grown to include almost every faith. Although you go through the process with other couples, most of your time is focused on your own marriage relationship.

The process involves writing each other a series of letters, beginning the first night with "What I really like about you is . . ." and ending on the last day with "Why I choose to spend the rest of my life with you." One spouse is asked to write his or her letter in the meeting room while the other person writes in the couple's hotel room. When the letter-writing time is up, the person in the meeting room goes back to the hotel room and, with a hug, exchanges letters with his or her spouse. After reading each other's letter, the couple decides who goes first. So, for instance, if I went first, I would tell Margie what she really liked about me most until she agreed that's what she had said in her letter. Then Margie would tell me what I really liked about her until I agreed that's what I had said. This was a wonderful way to make sure we had heard each other properly. After making sure we understood each other's feelings, we would talk.

At the end of the weekend, couples who had completed the process walked out with smiles on their faces and love in their hearts. The organizers suggested that we continue to use this letter-writing dialogue process in the future whenever issues crop up. Margie and I still use this method today. When an important issue comes up and we need to really understand each other's point of view, we get out the paper and pens and start writing.

Whatever strategies you employee to nurture your marriage—whether seeking marital counseling, attending workshops, writing letters, or something different altogether—keep your commitment to your commitment. Invest the effort and expense; it will be worth it. Marriage is the most important relationship you will ever have. Margie and I are more in love with each other than ever before. What a blessing!

———— ❧ ————

Dr. Ken Blanchard is an author, speaker, and management expert who has coauthored more than thirty best-selling books. Ken is the Chief Spiritual Officer of The Ken Blanchard Companies, an international management training and consulting firm that he and his wife, Marjorie, cofounded in 1979. Their son, Scott, and daughter, Debbie, are Executive Vice Presidents for the company. Ken is also cofounder of Lead Like Jesus, a ministry devoted to helping people become servant leaders. Ken and Margie will celebrate their fiftieth anniversary in 2012.

2

Make Love a Verb

Andy Stanley

Falling in love is easy. It involves butterflies, long walks on moonlit beaches, and the occasional visit from a unicorn. There are fifteen hundred organizations in this country that will take your money and your profile and connect you with somebody with a similar profile. It has never been easier to fall in love.

But while *falling* in love is easy, I would argue that it's never been more difficult to *stay* in love. Once the initial shine of new love has worn off, there are obstacles that appear seemingly out of nowhere. There are warts, there are regrets, there is *baggage*. Sometimes, staying in love feels impossible.

Though the divorce statistics jump all over the place, there is little denying that we are a culture prone to giving up on love, instead of staying in it. We are a culture that believes that when the going gets tough, the tough just go.

9

We run away from the challenges and wonder how we could ever feel so far from someone we once felt so close to. The people we couldn't live without become the people we can't stand to be in the same room with.

Yet despite the challenges, there's something in you and in me that wants to do life and finish life with that special someone. We don't want to just be in a relationship; we don't want to just survive the years. We want to be *in love*. We wonder what it's like to be truly treasured by someone. To be needed and missed and loved. Not just for a long weekend or even a decade, but for twenty years, thirty years, forty years, and more.

LOVE IS A VERB

For many of us, the concept of love is difficult because we never really learned the right form of love.

The truth is, very few people have ever been around a healthy marriage relationship. Few of us grew up in homes where our parents were on the same page and had the kind of relationship we wanted to have one day. We didn't grow up with, "Do unto others as you would have them do unto you." We grew up with, "Do unto others as they did unto you." Or, "Do unto others until you wear them down and get your way."

In our homes, we weren't equipped to recognize real love, never mind replicate it someday in our own lives. So we developed low relational pain thresholds. We focus on the external qualities of love and ignore the internal. We treat love like a noun. It's an experience that happened. A moment. A thing.

But in John 13:34, we see a different side of love. Two thousand years ago Jesus gave us the best advice for staying in love. It's the foundation for enduring love relationships. It's so counterintuitive, so simple, it goes right over our heads. It's so powerful, so rare, so accessible, if two people will accept this very basic teaching of Jesus: "A new command I give you: Love one another." It will slip right by you if you're not careful. Jesus takes a word that we normally use as a noun and makes it a verb.

What Jesus was saying was, "I want you to learn how to actively love one another." Love is something you do. When two people actively love one another, guess what it does? It rekindles and continues to kindle, flame, enrich, and improve the "in love" part of the relationship.

It is not an event or a one-time thing. It is not a fireworks feeling or a field of flowers. It's an action. It's not just about *choosing* the right person; it's about *becoming* the right person—the type of person who loves the way Christ loved us. It's a daily commitment. But if it's going to happen, love must be a verb.

IT TAKES A PLAN

What if real relationships actually start when we get real about staying in love? What if staying in love is possible?

I believe it is possible. I believe it's a gift God longs to give us, and I believe there are three things we can do to accept that gift. Falling in love only requires a pulse. Staying in love? That requires a plan.

REMODEL YOUR APPROACH

For years, I've waged a steady opposition to my wife's plan to add a garden to our yard. I'm just not interested. If Sandra carves out some of her precious spare time and invests it in the garden, guess who doesn't get that time? So it's not just that I'm not interested in the garden; it might interfere with her priorities, one of which is *me*.

For a long time I had a good case going . . . and then I read Philippians 2:3 again: "Do nothing out of selfish ambition or vain conceit, but in humility consider others better than yourselves." I wish that were a complicated verse with multiple Hebrew variations. But when it comes to marriage, it's pretty simple. Value others, in this case your spouse, above yourself.

So now I have a decision to make: Am I going to love me? Am I going to talk her out of having a garden? Am I just going to ignore it and hope it goes away? The decision isn't whether I like gardening or whether I'm going to eat vegetables. It's bigger than that. The issue is whether I'm going to look to her interests or only to mine.

When you want to stay in love, you don't just put up with your loved one's interests. You find a way to become interested and express interest—just like you did before you got married. When you fell in love, you found out what your loved one was into and you suddenly, temporarily, were into it too. "Oh, I love to run." You'd never run in your life, but you went to your friend and said, "Do you have any running shoes that look used? I can't go out there with brand-new shoes." All of a sudden you were a runner.

See, we know how to *be* in love. But once we're in, we forget that we have to *stay* there. If you want to go deep, if you want real intimacy, then you live as if your loved one is more important than you—which means his or her interests become at least as important as yours.

If you want to go deep, if you want real intimacy,
then you live as if your loved one is more
important than you—which means his or her
interests become at least as important as yours.

Besides sharing their interests, how do you treat those who are more important than you? Let me tell you: you defer to them. You don't interrupt and say, "No, no. I think that was blue, not red." You don't pat them on the back and say, "Posture, posture." You laugh even when they're not funny. The key is respect, respect, respect. Through your actions, through what you say, through what you don't say, through the way you say it, you respect them and treat them as if they are more important than you.

To stay in love, you need to remodel your approach. You can try to draw the lines evenly so that you get a 50-50 split, but chances are that when you do, you will end up with a contract, not love. So learn to remodel. Learn to value others above yourself. Learn to put your spouse first. Learn to defer to your spouse. And remember: respect, respect, respect.

PAY ATTENTION TO YOUR HEART

It would be simple if we all came into marriage with backgrounds filled only with healthy relationships. Yet none of us do. We all bring baggage from relational hurts in our pasts. And that baggage will inescapably influence the way we experience our marriages. The emotional residue and repercussions from these difficult experiences in our pasts will inevitably spill out in the present as we hit various "bumps" in our marriage relationships.

Imagine you are a mug with thousands of tiny beads inside. Each bead represents a feeling or an experience or a hope or a fear. You are very careful to keep them inside. But then you meet her, and you think she just might be the future "Mrs. Mug." So, you are gentle and thoughtful around her. You both put your best foot forward and make certain that as few beads as possible spill out on the road to the altar.

Now it's a month or a year later, and suddenly there's an issue. She gets upset for no reason. You don't call, though you said you would. She feels ignored. You lose a promotion. Something in life blindsides you, and your mugs bump into each other. Jealousy spills out. Anger overflows. All the stuff that was hidden during the courtship is on display and it feels like there is nowhere to go from there. You stuff it down, but eventually it comes back up.

This is the type of situation the Bible predicts when it implores us to guard our hearts. Proverbs 4:23 says, "Above all else, guard your heart, for it is the wellspring of life." Your ability to feel certain things in certain ways is dependent on the condition of your heart. And if you don't guard it, if you don't protect it and monitor it, you'll never get a foothold on your feelings.

Your ability to feel certain things in certain ways is dependent on the condition of your heart.

In marriage, we guard our hearts by paying careful attention to what's going on inside us. We need a proactive strategy for doing this. We're good at monitoring our spouses' behavior, but we're horrible at monitoring what's really happening in our own hearts.

So what do you do when your marriage hits the inevitable bumps and your emotional beads spill out? Here's an exercise that can help:

1. Instead of stuffing your feelings or justifying them, stop and think about what you are actually feeling before you speak.
2. Name what you are feeling, with specific words: *I feel jealous or angry or left out. I feel like a failure.*

I feel abandoned, afraid, betrayed, disrespected, insecure.

3. Once you've identified the feeling, say it aloud. Name your feelings and they lose their power.
4. If and when it's appropriate, tell your spouse what's going on in your heart. And when your partner does this, the right way to respond is to simply say, "Thank you, I'm glad you told me."

It might be hard at first, but healthy people stop doing hurtful things when they learn what the issues are. And they stay in love by paying close attention to their hearts.

CHOOSE WISELY IN FILLING THE GAPS

In every relationship, there are gaps between what is expected and what actually happens. We have fairy-tale views of how marriage will be and it fails to deliver. We have expectations of how a spouse should act at a dinner party and that doesn't go as planned. We have secret beliefs about what time someone should come home at night and the reality is different. Gaps open up all around us. When that happens, we have two choices about how we fill them. We can believe the best. We can trust that there is an unexplained delay or something critical that came up to keep our spouses out late. Or we can assume the worst. We can read disrespect, hurt, and a thousand other things into those situations.

Into that powder keg, 1 Corinthians 13 walks boldly. Long used in weddings, these popular verses describe the nature of love. Beyond the verses about love's patience and kindness, we find a plea for the gaps. We find help for the holes. Verse 7 says love "always protects, always trusts, always hopes, always perseveres."

In a marriage, that means when you have a chance to doubt or trust, you trust. When you have a chance to give up or hope, you hope. When you have a chance to quit or persevere, you persevere.

Each time we experience a gap where our expectations aren't met, we face a choice: in our hearts and minds, will we assume the worst about our spouses, or believe the best? Husbands and wives who stay in love for the long haul learn to always assume the best, either by force of habit or by intuition. By doing so, they create an "upward spiral of love" leading to greater and greater intimacy.

MARRIAGE SPEAKS TO OUR CULTURE

Hopefully, this will be a start to a longer discussion about what it means to stay in love. It's not just better marriages that will exist at the end of this adventure. It's not just the chance to model a brand-new type of relationship for the next generation. As important as both of those things are, there's something even greater at stake.

Nothing speaks louder to our culture about Christianity than our marriage relationships. Marriage is not just love on display; it's also faith on display. And that's why we need to equip and encourage each other to *stay in love*.[1]

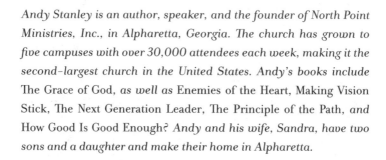

Andy Stanley is an author, speaker, and the founder of North Point Ministries, Inc., in Alpharetta, Georgia. The church has grown to five campuses with over 30,000 attendees each week, making it the second-largest church in the United States. Andy's books include The Grace of God, *as well as* Enemies of the Heart, Making Vision Stick, The Next Generation Leader, The Principle of the Path, *and* How Good Is Good Enough? *Andy and his wife, Sandra, have two sons and a daughter and make their home in Alpharetta.*

3

My Heavenly Father-in-Law

Gary Thomas

It came almost as a warning, and frankly, I needed one at the time. I was a young husband, and during an intense time of prayer, I sensed God telling me very directly that Lisa wasn't just my wife, that she was also His daughter and I was to treat her accordingly.

This was a moment of revelation for me, and the force of this insight grew once I had kids of my own. If you want to get on my good side, just be good to one of my kids. A wonderful young woman at our church became Allison's "big sister" when Ally was in her early teens, taking her out to Starbucks or for ice cream and being an overall positive influence. My wife and I will love Amy for the rest of our lives for the ways she was so generous and kind to one of our children.

Conversely, if you really want to make me angry, pick on my kids. Be mean to them. Bully them. My blood pressure will go up if your name is even mentioned. I'd much rather you mess with me than with one of my kids.

So when I realized I am married to *God's daughter*—and that you, women, are married to *God's sons*—my view of marriage completely changed. God feels about my wife—His daughter—in an even holier and more passionate way than I feel about my own daughters. Suddenly, my marriage was no longer about just me and one other person; it was very much a relationship with a passionately interested third Partner as well. In fact, I realized that one of my primary forms of worship throughout the rest of my life would be honoring God by taking care of a woman who would always be, in His divine mind, "His little girl."

We often hear pastors contemplate the fatherhood of God, a wonderful and true doctrine. But if you want to change your marriage, extend this analogy and spend some time thinking about God as your *Father-in-Law*. Because when you marry a believer, that's who He is!

If you want to change your marriage, spend some time thinking about God as your Father-in-Law.

When I fail to respect my wife, when I demean her or am condescending toward her, when I mistreat her in any way, I am courting trouble with the heavenly Father who feels passionately about my spouse's welfare.

"SHE'LL BE OKAY"

On the day my earthly father-in-law, Bill, died, he asked to speak to me on the phone. He had bravely fought cancer for nearly a decade and was tired. He wanted me to pray that God would let him go home soon.

My mind went back to our wedding rehearsal dinner, when Bill broke into tears telling me how happy he was about the next day's wedding. Bill wasn't overly emotional by any means, and almost two decades passed before he explained what was behind the tears: "Gary, when you married my daughter, I thought to myself, 'I don't have to worry about Lisa. She's going to be okay. She's found a guy who will take care of her.'"

Now that I have two daughters in their twenties, I know exactly what Bill was feeling. And so, during our last conversation, after we both shared some personal things, I told Bill, "I just want you to know how grateful I am that you gave me Lisa, and I want to remind you that you don't ever have to worry about Lisa. I'll make sure she's okay."

I said that because I can imagine that, on my own deathbed, that's exactly what I will want to hear. Secure about my eternal destiny—just as Bill was about his—I think I'll be most concerned about those I will be leaving behind. I'll want to know that someone will be there for my daughters.

Viewing God as Father-in-Law has helped me understand the apostle Peter's words: "Husbands, in the same way be considerate as you live with your wives, and treat them with respect as the weaker partner and as heirs with you of the gracious gift of life, so that nothing will hinder your prayers" (1 Peter 3:7).

If a young man came to me, praising me, complimenting me on my character, even singing songs about me and giving me monthly checks, and all the while I knew he was making one of my daughters miserable through abuse or neglect, I'd frankly have nothing to say to him except, "Hey, buddy, start treating my daughter better, and then we can talk." How he was treating my little girl would be the first and last thing I'd want to discuss until the situation changed. So it makes total sense to me that if I don't treat Lisa well, if I don't treat her with respect as God's daughter with all the honor and privileges such a high standing involves, my prayer life will be hindered.

GOD WANTS HIS KIDS TO BE LOVED

Seeing our spouses as God's sons or daughters also helps us love them despite their imperfections. I know my kids aren't perfect, but I still want them to be loved.

One summer I kiddingly told my son that I could write down the first three arguments he'd have with his future wife. I know him that well, and I know exactly where there is likely to be tension between him and a wife. At the time, he didn't even have a girlfriend, but when he did get one, their first disagreement was on my list.

Although I know where my son is likely to fail and even though I am fully aware of where my daughters are weakest and how they will most likely to try their spouses' patience, it's almost scary to me how desperately I want them to be loved. I want my son to find a woman who will honor, respect, and support him despite his weaknesses and sins. I want each of my daughters to find a man who will adore them, love them, and make them feel safe and secure even though at times they wake up with an attitude. None of my kids is perfect, but they'll always be my kids, which is why I'll always love the people who love them.

Is it any different with our heavenly Father-in-Law? God is fully aware of our spouse's limitations—and He is just as eager for us to be kind and generous with them despite these faults as we are for our kids' future spouses to be kind to them.

MARRIAGE: A CENTRAL PART OF OUR WORSHIP

Women, when you married that man and dreamed of long, soul-filled discussions late into the night, but six months after the wedding realized you married a man who wouldn't know an emotion if it bit him on the nose until he bled, think about your frustration in the context of this truth: you made a good God very, very happy by agreeing to love

His son despite all his limitations. Your disappointment is understandable, but your worship of God as evidenced in loving your husband anyway is a precious thing that will be rewarded in eternity.

Men, when you married that young woman, not realizing that breast cancer or Alzheimer's was in her future, and you want to say to yourself, "I didn't sign up for this!" consider how much joy you gave to your heavenly Father-in-Law when He could say on the day you got married, "I'm so pleased that Julie (or Katherine or Peggy) is with a good man who will stay with her and care for her out of reverence for Me. I know what's in their future, and I'll give this man what he needs. I just want him to take good care of My little girl."

When this is our attitude, marriage becomes a central aspect of our worship. We learn to love imperfect people by serving them out of reverence for our perfect God, who loves us despite our brokenness. "We love because he first loved us" (1 John 4:19).

We learn to love imperfect people by serving them out of reverence for our perfect God.

Most of us, however, fail to grasp just how fully God loves the person we married. Even if you spent ten years thinking about it, you'd still fall short of understanding how much God truly cares about your spouse. He designed and created your spouse. He wooed your spouse to regeneration.

He adores and feels passionately about the one you married. If any doubt remains as to His care and concern, consider this: He sent His only Son to die on behalf of your spouse.

Think about how you treated your husband or wife this past week. Is that how you want your son or daughter to be treated by his or her spouse? Never forget: you didn't just marry a man or a woman; you married a son or daughter of God.

Treat him, treat her, accordingly.

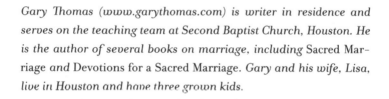

Gary Thomas (www.garythomas.com) is writer in residence and serves on the teaching team at Second Baptist Church, Houston. He is the author of several books on marriage, including Sacred Marriage *and* Devotions for a Sacred Marriage. *Gary and his wife, Lisa, live in Houston and have three grown kids.*

4

Practice Non-Random Acts of Kindness

Paul and Teri Reisser

I (Teri) arrived at adulthood with a firmly held belief that any relationship with someone of the opposite sex would inevitably become an ongoing game of carefully plotted strategies. This approach was, in part, the by-product of the way I was treated (or I should say mistreated) by men when I was a teenager, but this choice was also fueled by what I observed all too often at home when I was growing up.

Having not received a lot of nurturing when she was growing up, my mom (consciously or otherwise) developed a view that marriage required a permanent war room for carefully planning and tracking skirmishes with the "enemy" (aka my dad). She lost more battles than she won, but she became adept at the fine art of making the enemy pay dearly for his wins. She could punish with icy silence until he yielded in one way or another, and then she would return to the war room and move her pins around to a win position. I often imagine what kind of wonderful changes have taken place in their relationship, now that they have both graduated to a permanent home with God, a home where there are no war rooms or icy silences.

And then I met the woman who would become my mom-in-law.

Harriet was the mom everyone dreams of having. It was as if she had just walked off the set of *Leave It to Beaver*. Her guiding principle was service—to her husband, her children, her grandchildren, her community, her church. Her straightforward sense of self—she was thoroughly comfortable both in her own skin and in her understanding of God's ownership of her life—freed her from the burden of thinking too long and hard about protecting her "rights." She had a work ethic the size of Montana. She reached optimal joy and satisfaction in life when those under the umbrella of her care were relaxed and laughing and loving because of her ministrations.

Harriet never sat me down and lectured me about how to take care of my husband (aka "her only and beloved son"). She didn't have to because I took careful note of the abundant fruit resulting from the way she treated others. She put everyone else's comfort ahead of her own—without being a doormat. (She was very capable of taking care of herself.) In turn, we all looked for ways to lighten *her* load.

Don, my dad-in-law, clearly adored his wife. I don't know who started the pattern, but by the time I arrived on the scene, I observed two people who treated each other with small kindnesses that transmitted a clear message: "You are not the enemy. You are my friend, and I care about your load. How may I make your life easier today?"

PAUL'S STORY

My (Paul's) dad was a World War II veteran who had never finished college. He wanted both of his kids to go as far with their education as they could without any hindrance, financial or otherwise. In my case, "otherwise" included getting too involved with someone before I finished with school, and he often issued somber warnings about marriage derailing one's education. He became concerned when it was clear that Teri and I were getting serious during my last year of medical school, and on two occasions he exhorted her not to marry me. This was the only miscalculated advice he ever gave us, and we politely declined it, having received unqualified approval of our marriage plans from many others who knew us well. (I should add that once the wedding day arrived, he offered unqualified support for us as a couple.) What he hadn't realized was how well he had, by his example, prepared us for marriage.

My father had a well-defined "I'm the head of the house" mentality that was thoroughly tempered by a servant's heart when it came to my mom. I watched him treat her with respect and generosity day in and day out, in more ways than I can count or name. Not at all bound by any formula regarding what was a man's work or a woman's work in the home, he readily pitched in to clear a table, polish

the utensils, or rev up the vacuum cleaner when the occasion required. He showed me how to wipe down the bath-
room sink after I used it and expected me to do so as well.
He always opened doors for my mom, and he taught me to
do likewise when I began to go out on dates. My dad also
made it abundantly clear how I was to conduct myself with
girls and women at a time (in the late 1960s) when moral
boundaries were literally evaporating.

Lessons like these were second nature by the time I
met Teri, with whom I had the unique experience of enjoying ridiculously easy communication and "Where have you
been all my life?" attraction from our magical first date. I
couldn't believe that I was somehow appealing to such a
beautiful and intelligent woman, and neither my dad nor I
could have predicted how my following his example would
affect her.

TERI'S STORY, PART II

Because of what my in-laws had modeled for Paul, from
our first conversation onward I was struck by the level of
his thoughtfulness and how naturally it seemed to flow from
him. This kind of warm regard was a new concept for me: I
found myself on the receiving end of small acts of kindness
that were done "just because I value you," not as a maneu-
ver calculated to achieve some specific end. Needless to say,
I didn't find Paul's warm consideration of me at all hard to
get used to or to reciprocate during the bloom of romance
and early marriage.

But all of us are selfish creatures by nature, so it is much too easy to get used to having someone serve us. And, worse, it's quite easy to feel entitled to that kind of care or take it for granted. Furthermore, the demands of daily responsibilities can effectively erode our impulses to serve our spouse, especially when we're exhausted or frustrated by what kids, a job, and life pile on our plate every day. Paul and I both have overly ambitious schedules, and we have found that these frequently increase our self-absorption as we race against the clock to check off our assorted punch lists. It would be nice if small kindnesses would happen automatically while we were contending with whirlwind agendas. But, like virtually anything else that's important in life, those kindnesses require a focused, intentional discipline.

Like virtually anything else that's
important, non random acts of kindness
require focused, intentional discipline.

OUR CONCLUSIONS

Every day a couple can find literally dozens of occasions to send one of two messages: either "I value you, so I took a minute to take care of this for you" *or* "Life is tough, kid! Fend for yourself because I'm too busy to be bothered!" To help you choose the former, we offer these examples of small kindnesses from our household:

- Changing the roll of toilet paper *or* seeing how little toilet paper you can use, so the other person has to deal with that springy holder thing.
- Twisting that blasted plastic ring off the new gallon of milk *or* using less milk on your cereal in order to leave the finger-gouging task for your spouse.
- Taking out the full kitchen trash bag *or* cramming in one more item and hoping that your spouse will haul that heavy, smelly, overflowing bag out to the garbage container.
- Taking fifteen seconds to turn down your spouse's side of the bed and turn on his/her reading lamp *or* just plopping your weary body into bed.
- Refilling the sugar bowl *or* putting a little less sugar in your coffee just so you don't have to pull that bag out of the pantry, struggle to replenish the bowl, and clean up the mess you made on the counter when the bowl overflows.
- Picking up a dirty saucer or glass from where the other has been working or relaxing *or* "teaching" your spouse (with a nice discontented sigh) to take his/her own dirty dishes to the sink.
- Offering to refill the other person's coffee cup *or* making your spouse get some much-needed exercise (i.e., walking to the kitchen).

The list is potentially endless, and, while any one of these items might seem trivial, their impact over time can be monumental. Obviously, if only one person is performing small acts of kindness without reciprocation, the person being served can develop a sense of entitlement, and the person serving can become resentful. But when two people are consistent and intentional about looking out for each other in these simple ways, a powerful message is both sent and received: "I am a witness to your life. I see these routine things that are part of your daily grind, and I want to lighten your load in this small way to show you how much I love you."

This is literal money in the relational bank. Deposits may be made at any time. "Give generously, for your gifts will return to you later" (Ecclesiastes 11:1, NLT).

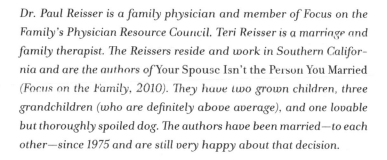

Dr. Paul Reisser is a family physician and member of Focus on the Family's Physician Resource Council. Teri Reisser is a marriage and family therapist. The Reissers reside and work in Southern California and are the authors of Your Spouse Isn't the Person You Married *(Focus on the Family, 2010). They have two grown children, three grandchildren (who are definitely above average), and one lovable but thoroughly spoiled dog. The authors have been married—to each other—since 1975 and are still very happy about that decision.*

5

Lighten Up and Laugh

Ted Cunningham

Enjoy life with your wife, whom you love,
all the days of this meaningless life
that God has given you under the sun—
all your meaningless days.
For this is your lot in life and in your
toilsome labor under the sun.

—Ecclesiastes 9:9

Preacher Henry Ward Beecher is attributed with saying, "A [marriage] without a sense of humor is like a wagon without springs—jolted by every pebble in the road. Humor makes all things tolerable."

"Laugh out loud," says Chuck Swindoll. "It helps flush out the nervous system." On another occasion Chuck said, "Laughter is the most beautiful and beneficial therapy God ever granted humanity."

Psychoanalyst Martin Grotjahn, author of *Beyond Laughter*, notes that "to have a sense of humor is to have an understanding of human suffering."

Bob Hope called laughter an "instant vacation."

Jay Leno is attributed as saying, "You can't stay mad at somebody who makes you laugh."

Bill Cosby says, "If you can find humor in anything, you can survive it."

In her book *Americans and Others*, essayist and biographer Agnes Repplier, who was known for her common sense and good judgment, wrote, "We cannot really love anybody with whom we never laugh."

I agree with all of the above. Their cumulative wisdom is the basis for the best advice for marriage I can imagine: lighten up and laugh!

LIGHTEN UP!

I've often wondered, "What if we all get to heaven and find out there were more than five love languages?" I love and respect Dr. Gary Chapman, but I think he forgot one because *laughter* is my love language. One of my missions in life is making Amy Cunningham laugh. She is my best friend, and we spend lots of time laughing together. Not taking yourself so seriously is the first step toward bringing laughter into your marriage. Being a responsible adult does not mean that you must remain serious at all times.

Most people would point to Ephesians 5 as the primary marriage text of the Bible, but to do so overlooks a major Old Testament nugget about marriage. I get that we are to lay down our lives for our wives, guys, but I think God never intended for us to choose between our life and our wife. Solomon said that we can and should enjoy both.

Many marriage books and ministries emphasize that God gives us a spouse to make us more like Jesus. While marriage can make us more like Jesus, we must not forget that God created marriage prior to sin entering the world. The creation order establishes the priority of marriage as companionship, not sanctification (Genesis 2:18). God wants you to *enjoy* your marriage.

The creation order establishes the priority of marriage as companionship, not sanctification. God wants you to enjoy *your marriage.*

LIFE IS A GRIND

Life is hard, you die, and then you're forgotten. This is a theme of Ecclesiastes. You can see why people avoid this book—it's too depressing! But if you mine the nuggets of Ecclesiastes, you will begin to see God's heart for your life and marriage.

In Ecclesiastes 1, word pictures from creation are used to explain our life on this planet. And, as it is described here, life on this earth is a total grind:

The words of the Teacher, son of David, king
in Jerusalem:

"Meaningless! Meaningless!"
    says the Teacher.
"Utterly meaningless!
    Everything is meaningless."

What does man gain from all his labor
    at which he toils under the sun?
                    (Ecclesiastes 1:1–3)

We are born into this grind called life, and the churning begins. We face hard times and challenges all through life. In our young marriage we understand the grind soon enough. We probably experienced the grind the most in trying to make a living. It may have gotten very hard. We may have felt the grind when our career pursuits don't go as planned or when we tried to pay bills with an already stretched bank account. The Bible says the grind continues all the way until the end:

The length of our days is seventy years—
    or eighty, if we have the strength;
yet their span is but trouble and sorrow,
    for they quickly pass, and we fly away.
                    (Psalm 90:10)

Age will not get us out of the grind. Even if we make it to eighty years of age, our life will be tough. In this text, *trouble* and *sorrow* mean gruesome, difficult, and painful, and it's a myth to think that the more years we get under our belt, the easier the grind will get. Money cannot buy our way out of it. Academic degrees cannot outsmart it. Age and maturity won't deliver us from pain and trials.

In fact, Solomon actually said the grinder will eventually take over our body. I love to read Ecclesiastes 12:1–5 to Amy at night to help us both picture our senior years on the front porch, rocking away:

> Remember your Creator
>> in the days of your youth,
> before the days of trouble come
>> and the years approach when you will say,
>> "I find no pleasure in them"—
> before the sun and the light
>> and the moon and the stars grow dark,
>> and the clouds return after the rain;
> when the keepers of the house tremble,
>> and the strong men stoop,
> when the grinders cease because they are few,
>> and those looking through the windows
>> grow dim;
> when the doors to the street are closed
>> and the sound of grinding fades;
> when men rise up at the sound of birds,
>> but all their songs grow faint;
> when men are afraid of heights
>> and of dangers in the streets;
> when the almond tree blossoms
>> and the grasshopper drags himself along

> and desire no longer is stirred.
> Then man goes to his eternal home
> and mourners go about the streets.

We're in the grind all the way to the end, and our only way out of the grind is death. Are you encouraged yet? Life is hard, and then we die. Why in the world are you still reading this chapter?

We become fragile, and our bodies start breaking down. We lose our teeth. Our glasses will get thicker and thicker as we begin to lose our eyesight. We will stay inside the house, and the sounds of the marketplace will grow faint to us. We'll nap all day long and wake up every morning at 3:00 AM. Walking will be difficult for fear of stumbling. Your almond tree will blossom, which means your hair will turn gray. (At thirty-six, I am already experiencing this.) Then right before death, sex will become difficult if not impossible. The grasshopper starts dragging. Sexual desire is no longer stirred.

LIVE LIFE AND ENJOY IT!

In the midst of the grind, God still wants us to enjoy life: "Go, eat your food with gladness, and drink your wine with a joyful heart, for it is now that God favors what you do. Always be clothed in white, and always anoint your head with oil" (Ecclesiastes 9:7–8).

You and I have a responsibility in the daily grind to play and have fun. Yes! God wants you to enjoy life and marriage!

In the midst of the grind that is life, while you're still alive, go and do something. Live life and enjoy it! You need to find and hold on to those moments—sharing a meal, laughing, and being joyful. Don't throw that out the window because life is difficult. We can do nothing to escape the grind. So, in the meantime, choose joy. And for goodness sake, let's not pretend that our spouse is the reason for the grind.

God did not give me my spouse as part of the grind; rather, Amy and I are going through the grinder of life together. In the same way, you do not have to choose between life and a spouse. You can enjoy life with your spouse in the midst of the grind: "Enjoy life with your wife, whom you love, all the days of this meaningless life that God has given you under the sun—all your meaningless days. For this is your lot in life and in your toilsome labor under the sun" (Ecclesiastes 9:9).

Notice it does not say, "Endure life with your wife all your miserable days." This is the only place in the Bible where it says, "Enjoy life with your wife." You and I do not need to choose between the two, and one does not trump the other. You can have both because marriage enhances life.

I love hearing guys tell me, "I had all sorts of plans, dreams, and goals for the future, but then I got married" or "My wife and I had all sorts of plans, dreams, and goals for the future, but then we had kids." Let me give you the Greek/Hebrew term for those statements: *hogwash!* Your spouse is not brought into your life to kill your fun, play, dreams, and goals. And your kids were not brought into your life to be a killjoy in your life either.

THERE'S A SEASON FOR EVERYTHING

The grind will have its seasons just as the earth does. Spring, summer, autumn, and winter will come in a marriage, although not like clockwork the way the seasons do in nature. God created the earth on a 23.5-degree axis and placed it in perfect rotation around the sun. Hence the seasons. Here in Branson, Missouri, we experience all four seasons, though some more extreme climates may only offer two: dry and rainy. Whatever the case, the seasons do not last forever in nature.

Similarly, seasons in a marriage do not last forever. But enjoying marriage—enjoying life—is only possible when we grasp the concept of seasons, when we recognize the truth that we will experience many seasons in life and in our marriage, and that none of them will last forever. Amy and I have had a lot of different seasons in our marriage. The newborn and toddler seasons were tough, but they quickly turned to springtime. The seminary season was a tough one financially, but it too turned to spring once I graduated and earned some money to pay bills. My first few years as a senior pastor were the toughest season of our marriage, but we stuck it out and have enjoyed many springs since. Seasons create a pace and rhythm that breathe hope into a marriage. Thank You, Father, for seasons!

Our marriages need to be refreshed with regularity. It is the season of laughter:

There is a time for everything,
and a season for every activity under heaven:
a time to be born and a time to die,
a time to plant and a time to uproot,
a time to kill and a time to heal,
a time to tear down and a time to build,
a time to weep and a time to laugh,
a time to mourn and a time to dance.

(Ecclesiastes 3:1–4)

Laugh in the midst of the grind, and remember not to take yourself too seriously. Proverbs 17:22 says, "A cheerful heart is good medicine." Your marriage needs several good doses of this medicine. Don't keep it hidden away and stored in the medicine cabinet. Thank You, Lord, for the gift of laughter. Now go! Enjoy life with your spouse!

Ted Cunningham is the founding pastor of Woodland Hills Family Church in Branson, Missouri. He is the author of Trophy Child *and* Young and In Love *and is the coauthor of four books with Dr. Gary Smalley. Ted speaks each month with Gary Smalley on his national* Love and Laughter *marriage conferences. Ted and his wife, Amy, live in Branson with their children, Corynn and Carson.*

6

Be Your Partner's Best Friend

Les and Leslie Parrott

Two days after our wedding in Chicago, Les and I were nestled into a cottage surrounded by towering timbers along the picturesque Oregon Coast. A few miles to the south of us were the famous coastal sand dunes where we planned to ride horses later that week. And up the coast was a quaint harbor village where we thought we might spend another day leisurely looking at shops and eating our dinner by candlelight in a rustic inn some friends had recommended. Other than that, we had nothing on our itinerary for the next five days except enjoying the beach and each other, rain or shine.

Neither of us could have dreamed up a better setting for our honeymoon. Not that everything was perfect. We accidentally locked ourselves out of our rental car the day after we arrived. I was commenting on how the sun was trying to poke its way out of some clouds when Les realized that the keys were in the ignition and all the doors were locked.

"You stay here in the cabin," Les said, taking his first stab at being an everything's-under-control husband. "I'm going to walk to that filling station on the main road and get some help."

"I'll go with you," I responded.

"Are you sure? It might rain."

"It'll be fun. Let's go."

We talked as we walked the two or three miles to the pay phone (this was before cell phones), where we made arrangements for the locksmith to pick us up and take us back to our car. Sitting on a curb, we waited, saying nothing, while a couple of seagulls chatted it up overhead. Les was fiddling with a stick he'd picked up on our walk when I realized that several minutes had passed and neither of us had said a word. It was an easy stillness, however, a kind of eloquent voicelessness: we were content, comfortable with silence.

And I think it was there and then, quietly sitting on a curb next to a phone booth under a cloudy sky, that the thought hit me: I had captured true love. I'm not talking about mere romance or the excitement of passion. I'm talking about an abiding love that embraces deep affection and friendship. The thing I'd been chasing after ever since I was old enough to know it could be sought was now in my possession: I had married a man who loved me deeply, just as I loved him—and we were best friends. We had committed ourselves to walking together forever.

TRUE LOVE

Love's ethereal mysteries were now unfolding before my very eyes. Its elusive qualities were fading. True love was no longer out of reach. The very opposite, in fact, was true. While I stood by doing nothing, love was enveloping my being. Not in a heady sense. I'm not talking about the dizzying effects of falling in love that we experience in the early starry-eyed stages of a new relationship. Les and I had dated for nearly seven years before we were married and honeymooning on the Oregon Coast.

The love I'm talking about experiencing that day was clear-eyed and grounded in companionship. We were allies. Comrades. Partners. Companions. There was no sunset spiking our mood, no piped-in background music to romanticize the scene. This was the reality of being together as husband and wife not only in love, but in friendship.

THE SHELTER OF EACH OTHER

"It is not a lack of love," said Friedrich Nietzsche, "but a lack of friendship that makes unhappy marriages." World-renowned marriage researcher John Gottman, of the University of Washington, told us one day over lunch: "Happy marriages are based on a deep friendship." Being friends in marriage, it turns out, is critical to lifelong love. That's why we say it's the best advice we've ever gotten on marriage. By the way, this sage advice is not just a cute idea you might find on a plaque in a gift shop: lots of research and dozens of studies back it up.

Strangely, despite all the studies, not much has been written on the topic. You'll find countless volumes on romance, intimacy, and passion in marriage, but not much on the simple act of being good friends as husband and wife. It seems friendship is secondary to romance in the minds of many.

But get this: Gallup's research indicates that a couple's friendship quality could account for 70 percent of overall marital satisfaction. In fact, the emotional intimacy that a married couple shares is said to be five times more important than their physical intimacy.[1] So it stands to reason that we, as couples, can ignite our love life by boosting the quality of our friendship. It's advice every couple can follow.

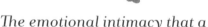

The emotional intimacy that a married couple shares is said to be five times more important than their physical intimacy.

HOW TO BECOME BETTER FRIENDS

Legend tells of a young Persian soldier asked by his king, Cyrus the Great, whether he would trade the horse on which he had just won a race for an entire kingdom. "Certainly not, sire," the young soldier replied, "but I would gladly part with him to gain a good friend."

A good friend is hard to find. And when we find one—particularly in marriage—we sometimes take that person for granted. Here are a few tips to keep from doing that.

Look through your partner's eyes

Barbara Brown Taylor, a professor at Piedmont College in rural Georgia, knows. "My husband, Edward," she writes, "is devoted to hawks and especially to the golden eagles that are returning to our part of Georgia. Driving down the highway with him can be a test of nerves as he cranes over the steering wheel to peer at the wing feathers of a particu larly large bird."

Her husband, like any bird enthusiast, wants to know whether it's an eagle or just a turkey vulture. In fact, as Barbara says, he *has* to know, even if it means weaving down the road for a while or running completely off the road from time to time. "My view," she continues, "is a bit different: 'Keep your eyes on the road!' I yell at him. 'Who cares what it is? I'll buy you a bird book. I'll even buy you a bird! Just watch where you're going!'"

A couple summers ago, Barbara and Edward's schedules kept them apart for two months, and she thought she'd get a break from eagles. "Instead I began to see them everywhere," she says, "looping through the air, spiraling in rising thermals, hunkered down in the tops of trees. Seeing them, really seeing them for the first time in my life, I understood that I was not seeing them with my own eyes but with Edward's eyes. He was not there, so I was seeing them for him."[2]

Barbara couldn't wait to tell her husband about the eagles she'd seen. Why? Because Edward had opened her eyes to what she wouldn't have seen without him.

Set your clock to friendship

We try to make it. Save it. Seize it. Buy it. And even borrow it. Yet time for each other continues to elude too many couples. But true friendship can't be built without it. Truman Capote said, "Friendship is a pretty full-time occupation." So true.

Most married couples live and love on borrowed time. They spend their prime time on everything "out there," and then scrape together whatever is left over and bank on the time they're borrowing from the future, saying, "Someday we'll do this or that . . . Tomorrow we won't be so busy . . . Eventually things will be different." But that's not good enough for good friends. Instead, good friends own outright each moment they have together: they are choosing to invest time in the relationship. And their calendar proves it. They schedule dates. They share meals. They book trips and adventures. If they don't set their watches for each other, they end up like far too many couples—being roommates rather than soul mates.

Study each other's funny bone

Some years ago we wrote a book called *The Love List*. It's designed to help couples do eight little things that make a big difference in their marriages. And of all the suggestions we note in this book, the chapter called "Find Something That Makes You Both Laugh" seems to resonate most with couples. And why shouldn't it? After all, laughter is essential to being good friends. It bonds people like nothing else can. Sure, you feel sad when your friend is sad. You shoulder his pain. But you also share his funny bone.

If you want to become better friends in your marriage, be sure to tickle each other's sense of humor on a regular basis. How? In any number of ways. Recall funny moments from your past that always make you laugh. If you're inclined, play a practical joke or watch a favorite sitcom or comedy. Everybody's funny bone is located in a different place. Some like the cerebral humor of Woody Allen while others enjoy the slapstick of the Three Stooges. Only the two of you know what really makes you laugh. So laugh often.

By the way, laughter is a literal healing balm for your marriage. It has important physiological effects on you and your spouse. Of course this isn't news. Since at least King Solomon's time, people have known about and applied the healing benefits of humor. As Proverbs tells us, "A cheerful heart is good medicine" (17:22). So study your spouse's funny bone and add more laughter into your relationship.

Protect each other's backs
When Richard Nixon was at the lowest ebb of the Watergate trials and nearing impeachment, he received a heartfelt letter from his friend Harold Macmillan, former prime minister of England. Years later, when Macmillan died, Nixon wrote a tribute to him and spoke of how meaningful that letter was. "What you learn when you fail," Nixon wrote, "is who your real friends are."

The same is true of couples in marriage. Good friends protect one another. They don't desert you, even when you are in trouble. And they don't desert you when it costs them something to remain your friend—even if that something is their pride. Some people call this trait faithfulness. Others call it loyalty or consistency. Whatever you call it, this trait is vital to the friendship of a husband and wife.

Think about it. Everyone, at some time or another, enters a dark day and walks alone. We all experience our own private Gethsemane. We all suffer loss. We encounter pain and deep disappointments. It is in these desperate times that we can watch one another's backs, protecting one another from harm.

And even when we somehow create our own harm in marriage, when fighting is becoming too commonplace, it's time to lean in to this friendship quality all the more. In a recent survey asking the question, "What would make you leave your spouse?" nearly a third of the more than six thousand respondents said, "Chronic fighting."[3] But fighting need not be an issue, because good friends rally around one another. They have one another's backs. And then—in Jesus' words—there is this, perhaps the greatest sign of friendship there is: "Greater love has no one than this, that he lay down his life for his friends" (John 15:13).

YOUR WELLSPRING IN THE WILDERNESS

Marriage is a wilderness if you're not good friends. We fervently believe investing in your friendship with your spouse will make a significant impact on the health of your marriage. Of course, like any other friendship, we can sometimes take for granted—like a well-worn pair of boots—our friendship with our spouse. That's when following these tips is most important. And you know they're paying off when the friend you saw at breakfast is the same friend you can't wait to see when you come home at night. We are to be loyal to this friendship more than any other. And though we do sometimes take it for granted, may we never want to trade it for anything.

1. Tom Rath, *Vital Friends: The People You Can't Afford to Live Without* (New York: Gallup Press, 2006), 29.

2. Barbara Brown Taylor, *The Best Spiritual Writing*, ed. Phillip Zaleski (San Francisco: Harper, 1999), 262).

3. Michelle Healy, "Deal Breakers," *USA Today* (April 27, 2010).

Drs. Les and Leslie Parrott are number-one New York Times bestselling authors and founders of LesandLeslie.com. They are also founders of the Center for Relationship on the campus of Seattle Pacific University and pioneered marriage mentoring (Marriage MentorSite.com). Their award-winning books include Saving Your Marriage before It Starts, The Complete Guide to Marriage Mentoring, *and* Love Talk.

7

Communicate How Much Your Mate Means to You

H. B. London

Fifty-four years ago, before there was a lot of marriage counseling, Jim Dobson (my uncle) married Beverley and me. On the wedding day, as we were sitting in the motel, he asked us, "What would you like to know? What do you want me to tell you?"

"Are you kidding?" I said. "I don't even know the questions to ask."

He just looked at me and said, "Well, okay. Here's my best advice: Don't ever go to sleep mad at each other. You need to stay awake until you get it all settled."

What Uncle Jim knew was that if we don't quickly address the issue at hand, then other issues will arise and morph into much bigger problems. So I've always tried to live by Ephesians 4:26-27: "'In your anger do not sin:' Do not let the sun go down while you are still angry, and do not give the devil a foothold." Please note I said, "I've always *tried.*" At times, I've tried and failed.

Although I'm far from perfect, I am nevertheless absolutely convinced that the failure to communicate honestly will, in time, lead to much more complicated issues. Deal with your issues as they happen or they will come to control you.

> *The failure to communicate honestly will,
> in time, lead to much more complicated
> issues. Deal with your issues as
> they happen or they will control you.*

DON'T MAKE ASSUMPTIONS

Beyond the usual interpretation of Ephesians 4:26, I think Uncle Jim was also saying to me, "Don't let your mate get the feeling that she's not valued or appreciated." I believe the key in avoiding that is attempting to keep the channel of communication open so that each of you can know what the other spouse is thinking as much of the time as possible. It's when we start guessing how our spouse is feeling that we often make mistakes, not only in judgment but also in verbiage. We start assuming what his or her needs are. Often our assumptions are based on what we want to hear rather than on reality.

LEARN HOW TO SHOW LOVE

In the early days of our marriage, Beverley would often ask me, "Do you love me? Do you love me? Do you love me?" At times it almost irritated me. It was frustrating. At twenty years old, I could say, "I love you," but I didn't know what to do beyond that. I am not sure I even understood what real love was. As a result, I probably created some insecurity in her because I didn't know how to affirm her as I should or express the love she needed.

Over the years I have had to make a concerted effort to learn how to show my wife that I loved her. But, at twenty-one, Beverley became a pastor's wife. Furthermore, I was an overachiever who traveled a lot. She had to deal with my being gone much of the time and raising our two sons by herself. I tried to find ways to take her away from her responsibilities and give her a break—going out to dinner or taking a trip or buying her something. I wanted to find ways to say, "You've been awfully patient, and you've been really kind through all of this. I just don't want you to ever think that I'm neglecting you or taking you for granted." I would also try to say this in so many words because Beverley needed to hear it from me.

Since then, I have learned that a lot of men just don't know how to say the things that need to be said when they need to be said. Many of us have come out of brokenness and fatherlessness, and we have never learned how to love or be compassionate. So, honestly, a lot of men who play softball four nights a week and then go out with the guys after the

game find that more fun than going home to three screaming kids and an unhappy wife. This choice leaves their wives
feeling unwanted, disrespected, and, at times, hopeless.

DON'T TAKE EACH OTHER FOR GRANTED

We husbands and wives can all too easily begin to take each
other for granted; we fail to express the kind of continued
affirmation that people need to hear. At times I take Bev for
granted even though I know better. Just the other day she
looked at me and said, "You didn't hear one word I said, did
you?"

I said, "To be honest with you, no, I didn't. I heard
noise, I heard a voice, but I didn't hear one word. I mean,
if you put a gun to my head and ask me to tell you what you
just said, I wouldn't be able to. But please don't put the gun
to my head." Fortunately, she didn't. We laughed.

One thing I've always told young couples is
to not be afraid to ask each other questions.

One thing I've always told young couples is to not be
afraid to ask each other questions. Even simple questions
like "How are you doing?" will yield a lot of information if
you listen to the answer. Often, if a spouse is feeling lonely
or fearful or frustrated, he or she just needs a chance to tell
you. But often we don't want to know because we will have

to make changes in our attitude and our actions. However, even if we do not want to know how our spouse is doing, we need to ask.

We can develop what I call "creative listening," which means we hear what we want to hear—and it's not necessarily what was said! For instance, your spouse might say to you, "I've been trying to tell you for two weeks now that I'm overwhelmed and feeling neglected, and you haven't heard me. For some reason, anything I've tried to say or do has gone right over your head. Why?"

When this happens, I often return to Uncle Jim Dobson's original advice: I can't allow myself to grow deaf to my spouse who's calling out for help or relief. When this happens, mates can develop a kind of independence. They'll say, "Okay. I'm going to have to find some way to feel fulfilled," or, "I'm going to have to find someone else who will listen when I talk." That new strategy causes an aloofness to develop in the relationship, and an affair can too easily happen. Loneliness often leads someone to lean on the shoulder of another person who will listen. So keep talking to your spouse—and never, never stop listening.

THE ROOT OF AFFAIRS

I've seen the consequences of this breakdown scores of times. Let's say a wife feels neglected and taken for granted. Both spouses work, so the woman goes to work and strikes up a friendship with a colleague that leads to some kind of emotional attraction. Then, because there are no real strings attached to this new relationship, both parties feel like they are communicating so easily. Perhaps they're being heard and affirmed; perhaps they're even feeling a sense of real value. And then they go home to the same old-same old and say, "You know, I like it better the other way." Divorce is not always the result, but a coolness that never thaws can definitely develop.

A lot of affairs occur because the person doesn't feel valued by his or her spouse or the marriage grows stale and boring. You have to really work at keeping a marriage alive and growing. Your marriage will not become routine if you keep loving each other, if you keep finding ways to refresh your love and your commitment to each other. The end result of not doing so is nearly always self-centeredness, and that will eventually lead to separation. Selfishness is a cruel thing, and Satan uses it in so many ways. It is the destroyer of relationships because it says, "My needs, my opinions, and my expectations are more important than my mate's."

TEN WAYS TO STOP COMMUNICATION

Over the many years that I've counseled couples, I've noticed ten things spouses can do that stop communication—and stopping communication is not good.

1. Being too busy: Acting on the sudden urge to mop the floor or wash the windows or cut the grass or

work on the car can cause just as much damage as staying at the office eighteen hours a day.

2. Staying away from home: Instead of facing the situation, the husband and wife keep time and space between them, passing each other like ships in the night.

3. Staying in the company of others: When we're surrounded by people, it's very easy to avoid the real issues. Often one spouse can become jealous of the other's friendships.

4. Do-goodism: This attempt to please people other than one's partner is a very insidious way of avoiding necessary conversation.

5. Sarcasm or ridicule: These forms of hostility hurt and harm their targets. So do words like *you never* or *you always*. Avoid those phrases!

6. Bringing up the past: Don't be historical. Face the present and move on.

7. Silence: The choice to not communicate implies that the other person is not worth sharing with, that you don't care what the other thinks, and that the other person has nothing to contribute.

8. Making the other person feel cheap or ignorant: Your spouse will never forget this.

9. Tools: Tactics like crying, slamming doors, screaming, going home to Mother, falling asleep, etc. will definitely prevent communication. When emotions are present, deal with them.

10. "What's the use?": Giving up when you should work at it accomplishes nothing. Too many marriages end prematurely because one or both parties just give up, apparently not finding the marriage worth saving.

Good communication, on the other hand, is being free to experience and express your true feelings as they arise. To do so is the basis for all growth-producing communication between husband and wife. Ephesians 4:29 says: "Do not let any unwholesome talk come out of your mouths, but only what is helpful for building others up according to their needs, that it may benefit those who listen." The important truth is that we can't unsay anything we say. We can never erase the things we say in moments of frustration or anger. Women especially tend to remember hurtful words forever.

The important truth is that we can't unsay anything we say.

IT TAKES A LIFETIME COMMITMENT

It took me a long time to figure out how to communicate with my wife, and I continue to try to tell her how much she means to me. I also pray for her and for us regularly. Prayer is a wonderful tool for ensuring that your marriage lasts a lifetime. When you pray for one another, God will enable you to keep strong what He has brought together.

Remember the power of a simple apology. It is amazing how the words "I'm sorry" can calm the waters. Finally, just keep talking and never stop listening. Do whatever you need to do to keep the channels of communication wide open. Love that communicates is love that never fails!

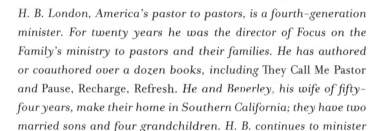

H. B. London, America's pastor to pastors, is a fourth-generation minister. For twenty years he was the director of Focus on the Family's ministry to pastors and their families. He has authored or coauthored over a dozen books, including They Call Me Pastor *and* Pause, Recharge, Refresh. *He and Beverley, his wife of fifty-four years, make their home in Southern California; they have two married sons and four grandchildren. H. B. continues to minister to pastors and their families through H. B. London Ministries. For further information, go to www.hblondon.org.*

8

Stop, Drop, and Roll

Dewey Wilson

What in the world were we thinking? I was lying in bed mulling over what had occurred a few hours earlier. The thoughts put a knot in my stomach that seemed the size of a bowling ball. My wife, Lynne, and I had just agreed to do something that clearly revealed our marriage was on shaky ground.

I admit that at times I'm a little slow to figure things out. In fact, some might say it takes me an hour and a half to watch *60 Minutes*. So when I initially agreed to the arrangement, I hadn't been worried. But now that the thought of sharing details of our sputtering marriage was becoming a reality, I started getting nervous. I asked myself, *What are we going to do?* Looking back, I should have realized the real question was, *What in the world is God about to do?*

THE REQUEST

What kept me up that night was a request by a couple in our church. James and Linda were only a few months away from their twentieth anniversary, but the past few years had been difficult for them. In fact, they were now living apart, the papers were signed, and the only thing keeping their divorce from becoming final was a judge's signature. However, James and Linda had discovered a last-chance option they thought might save their marriage.

While attending an anger management conference, James met a minister who suggested that they try finding a couple who had a good marriage and who they both respected. James and Linda were then to ask this couple to mentor them.

Well, they chose Lynne and me. I was their Bible Fellowship teacher, and Lynne seemed the ideal church leader's wife and mother. James and Linda invited us to dinner and popped the question: "Would you guys be willing to meet with us and share what works for you in your marriage?"

Lynne and I were only a few weeks away from celebrating our own twentieth anniversary. I was a successful residential homebuilder for one of the leading companies in Dallas. During this brief period in our marriage, Lynne was a stay-at-home mom, homeschooling our two teenage daughters. For most of our married life, in addition to homeschooling, Lynne had diligently worked beside me overseeing the operations in the two construction companies we had previously owned. She also managed the oil and gas drafting company she owned.

When we weren't at work or homeschooling, you could find us at our church. I was proud to own the titles of Deacon Officer, Deacon, Committee on Committees Chairman, and faithful Bible Fellowship teacher in one of the largest churches in the United States. Lynne had become a respected leader in ministry to children and youth, but most of the time she served alongside me.

Looking at us, you'd say we had it all. We were successful in business and respected leaders in our church. Unfortunately, what you see on the outside doesn't always match what you would see at home—and that's what really counts. The truth was that, as successful, busy, and respected as we were, our marriage stank. Over the years we had come to the place where many well-intentioned couples end up: simply coexisting.

HEALTHY ONLY ON THE OUTSIDE

For years, Lynne had been asking me to go to counseling to help us deal with the issues that kept us from having the kind of marriage we looked like we had—the kind of marriage we really wanted. But I was prideful and hugely afraid of being exposed, so telling a counselor (or anyone else) about the problems we were having simply wasn't going to happen. We had become pros at hiding our mediocre marriage from the rest of the world, which was like trying to hide a turkey on the Thanksgiving table. We could put on our suits and smiles, walk out the door of our house, and convince the rest of the world we were happy. Apparently, we had even convinced James and Linda.

A PRAYING WIFE

Although our marriage was upside down in many ways, Lynne's prayer life wasn't. Even though I wouldn't consent to counseling, she didn't give up or get angry. Instead, she prayed for years that God would intervene in our mess. At that point Lynne seemed to have God's ear, because that's exactly what He was about to do.

Beginning in January 2002 and continuing through May of that year, we met every week with James and Linda. We had no detailed plan to follow, but what we did have was a solid knowledge of God's Word and an assessment tool that helped people understand their basic personality strengths.

What God did over the next few months to restore James and Linda's marriage and totally enrich ours was incredible. In fact, it impacted our lives so dramatically that we surrendered to full-time vocational ministry in November 2002 and cofounded a ministry called Marriage Mentors, which has touched marriages all across the country. What Satan meant for evil in the lives of two couples, God meant for good.

YOU CAN START OVER TOO

Because you've chosen to read this chapter, you're probably serious about making your marriage better. It could also be that your marriage is in the same place ours was years ago. If so, like us, your marriage didn't become unhealthy overnight. It took time. And, while we turned things around in a few months, it wasn't a single big thing that did it all at once. In the same way that a bunch of bad decisions over time had nearly ruined our marriage, it would take a bunch of good decisions over time for things to get better. But our marriage did move from empty to fulfilling—and so can yours.

In fact, Lynne and I would like to share some simple truths about marriage that are effective with couples whether they need a tune-up or a major overhaul. It's not that our story should be canonized or that if you do exactly what we did, you'll get exactly what we got. You're a unique person, and your marriage comes with its own history and challenges. But we know that God's Word blasts through any wall—and we believe that if you try these basic principles, you won't be disappointed.

PRINCIPLES THAT CAN HELP ANY MARRIAGE

If you haven't already, I encourage you to grab a pen or highlighter because this next sentence is foundational to everything that follows—and it's the first thing to underline or highlight: Before change will occur in any person's life, he or she must first see that it makes sense to change.

Before change will occur in any person's life, he or she must first see that it makes sense to change.

Change needs to make sense

Shortly after we began mentoring James and Linda, Lynne and I realized that we couldn't impart what we didn't possess. So we knew that if we ever stood a chance at helping our friends, certain aspects of our marriage had to change. We started with changing our attitude toward each other's involvement in the mess.

For years, I'd had conversations with myself regarding just how inadequate Lynne had become at recognizing *my needs* and identifying *my desires*. At some point, me and myself took a vote and unanimously determined that our lack of happiness in marriage was all Lynne's fault. That didn't seem to matter much because she and herself must have taken the same vote and unanimously determined the same about us. So fitted with those lenses, Lynne and I became critical of almost everything the other did or didn't do in our marriage.

Yet now, because our friends needed our help, it was time for me to understand that regardless of how bad I perceived our marriage to be, Lynne alone was not responsible for the mess. I was responsible too. I'd like to report that

I had instant success in fully implementing this newfound truth, but I can't. Let's just say the *want* to change my attitude often exceeded my ability to follow through.

"*Stop, drop, and roll*"

The only change some people like is the kind that comes from the person at the drive-through window. Changing old habits and adopting new philosophies can be difficult, especially when you're so comfortable doing the very thing that needs to change. Well, here's something Lynne and I used to overcome our perceived inability to implement new changes. Not only has this worked for us, but it has also worked for countless numbers of people we've taught over the years. Each time Lynne and I felt the desire to react in a negative way or revert to stinkin' thinkin', we would simply remember to stop, drop, and roll. That's right: the same thing you were taught to do in elementary school if your clothes ever caught on fire. Here's what we mean.

Having old thoughts, which trigger old emotions, didn't cause most of our problems. But allowing those old emotions to drive our actions definitely caused problems. Scripture tells us in 2 Corinthians 10:4 that God has given us weapons that can help us destroy negative thinking. However, it's up to us to *stop* and take our negative thoughts captive.

Second in the sequence, *drop* symbolizes prayer, the next action needed. Regardless of whether you're seasoned at praying or not sure where to begin, if you take a few seconds to ask the Lord to help you, He can calm you down and defuse your negative emotions.

Third, *roll* invites you to get in the habit of replacing negative thoughts and actions with positive thoughts and actions. Just as rolling over and over on the ground smothers flames that could lead to death, our marriage began coming back to life when we stopped responding as we had in the past, started taking captive our negative thoughts toward each other, and, with God's help, started choosing to assume that the other person was speaking and acting with positive intentions. Interestingly, when we slowed down enough to practice this, something happened in both of us: we began to remember once again the things that made us fall in love with each other in the first place.

Become a student of your spouse

We had a tool to help us take this important step. The assessment that Lynne and I took confirmed what I already knew about myself: my personality drives me to be an assertive leader, fairly optimistic, and convincing. But—and I didn't especially like seeing this in black and white—I can be demonstrative, impulsive, impatient, independent, and pretty much self-willed.

And as you might have already imagined, Lynne is a little different from me. Her assessment revealed that she is predominantly cautious, hesitant, warm, convincing, and sociable. She is also predictable, resistant to change, systematic, and exacting. When I stopped valuing her God-given characteristics and started criticizing them as weaknesses, she began doing the same with mine. Our relationship began to spiral downward.

But over time, with God's help, I learned to become pretty good at taking my thoughts captive and not responding in ways that hurt Lynne. That was huge for me. Then, when I started taking my focus off what she wasn't giving me or doing for me and started recognizing and valuing her God-given qualities, the Lord quickly started bringing our marriage back to life. We did have something good to impart to James and Linda, but had God not answered Lynne's prayers the way He did, I am quite certain James and Linda would be divorced, our marriage would still be stuck in a rut, and countless relationships would still be giving way under Satan's power to destroy.

Lynne and I continue to be students of each other. We have to work at valuing each other's differences every day. Some days it requires more effort and emotional real estate than we want to give. But we are here to affirm the truth of Hebrews 11:6: "Without faith it is impossible to please [God], for he who comes to God must believe that He is, and that He is a rewarder of those who diligently seek Him" (NKJV).

GOD'S GOOD PLAN

You might not believe this statement today, but God *does* want what is best for you. However, for you to experience His best will first require faith on your part to believe that He does and then corresponding actions in response to that faith. I was once told, "Whatever you value you'll feed, and whatever you continually feed will eventually dominate you." One reason our marriage is strong today is because we continue to value each other and we make solid efforts to meet each other's needs. But maybe more important, our marriage is strong because we've come to know that God's plan for marriage, laid out in Scripture, works.

While we would like to share much more of what we've learned, remember that your attitude often determines your response, so we suggest you analyze your attitude first.

We also encourage you to remember to "stop, drop, and roll." When your emotional buttons are pushed in a negative way, take your thoughts captive, say a quick prayer, and choose to respond in a different way. If you want something to be different, you must do something different.

Finally, like us, if you and your spouse work to become a student of each other and to value each other's differences, we are quite certain God will begin doing an amazing work in you and in your marriage. After all, He wants to do "exceedingly abundantly above all that we ask or think, according to the power that works in us" (Ephesians 3:20, NKJV). We know that's His plan for you and your family. We pray you'll make it yours too!

------------ ❧ ------------

Dewey and Lynne Wilson started Marriage Mentors (www.marriage mentors.org) in 2002. Marriage Mentors is a successful nonprofit organization that operates through the financial gifts, prayers, resource income, and volunteer efforts of people and organizations who want to reverse the current trend of divorce in our society. The Wilsons have two grown daughters and make their home in Texas.

9

The Art of Affirmation

Joni Eareckson Tada

One Sunday my husband, Ken, and I came home from church. I thought we'd have a leisurely and lazy afternoon, as was our custom. But not long after I got into the house, I heard something rumbling down the driveway. It was the familiar sound of Ken moving our trash cans. *What's he putting them curbside for?* I wondered. *The trash truck doesn't come until tomorrow morning.*

I wheeled outside to investigate. Ken had already put the three big receptacles, filled to overflowing, out on the curb. The way I was raised, no one put trash cans out on the street on a Sunday afternoon. Sure, some of our neighbors would roll out their trash cans after the sun went down, but Ken had done it in daylight! I had to catch my husband before he dusted off his hands and finished the job.

"Ken, it's Sunday!" I called out. "It's way too early to put out our trash."

"What difference does it make?" he asked.

"Well, it makes a difference to me . . . and probably to our neighbors too," I replied. "It's what our family always did on Sunday."

He gave me a look of confusion.

"It's the same reason we don't hang out laundry on Sunday," I explained.

"We have a dryer, Joni. We *never* hang out laundry."

Before we knew it, our discussion spiraled into a head-on quarrel—which desecrated the Sunday far more seriously than a couple of trash cans on the curb did. I felt awful. What had begun as a beautiful, restful day had instantaneously degenerated. Now a stony wall of silence stood between my husband and me . . . and our garbage remained curbside.

Later that evening, as we were patching things up, we recalled the message we'd heard at church that very morning. It was from Matthew 12:36 where Jesus warned, "I tell you that men will have to give account on the day of judgment for every careless word they have spoken." How judgment and mercy will play out in heaven, I have no idea. Even though Christians will be shown grace, the verse *does* underscore the incredible importance God places on our every word. I realized there was a lot more carelessness in my Sunday lecture about garbage than I was at first quick to admit. And I was certainly careless about the things I spat out during our quarrel.

The "trash can argument" (as we have come to call it) happened early on in our marriage. But the experience and the advice from the sermon that day taught me a lesson for life. Since those early days, I've made it a habit to watch my words. Scripture has lots to say about our bodies, but no body part gets quite the attention as the tongue. For example, Proverbs 18:21 says, "The tongue has the power of life and death, and those who love it will eat its fruit." With our words we either beat the life out of our marriage *or* we cultivate, feed, and water it to ensure happy years ahead.

With our words we either beat the life out of our marriage or we cultivate, feed, and water it to ensure happy years ahead.

We women (and men too) wield incredible power when we speak. As a quadriplegic married to a strong, able-bodied man, I've learned a lot about this power over the decades. I may not be able to whip up an omelet for Ken or rub his back, I may not be able to fold his laundry or go fishing with him, but I *can* uplift him with words that give life, hope, and encouragement. I can applaud him, show appreciation, shower accolades when deserved, and let everyone know how proud I am of him. I may not be able to hold Ken's hand, but years ago I purposed to be his *best* cheerleader.

WHAT IS AFFIRMATION?

When I began the daily practice of affirming my husband, I was careful not to jump right in with mere flattery about superficial things. By affirmation, I don't mean sweet-talking to get my way or offering those precisely timed phrases that manipulate. By affirmation, I mean speaking sincere words that build him up.[1]

The other day, I saw him take a newspaper up to the door of our neighbor who recently had surgery. When he returned, I was quick to say, "Ken, *thank you* for doing that. You showed real thoughtfulness." How was I building him up? By commending him for the godly character qualities of attentiveness and kindness.

Here's another example. Over the years, I've observed that Ken is quick to invite people to pray as a group. Many times after a dinner date with friends, I've said, "Ken, I'm so grateful you're a man of prayer. God bless you for taking the lead at the close of that dinner and inviting people to pray. Good on you!" Never have I seen a man respond so warmly to encouraging words.

Even if the good you see in your spouse
seems infinitesimally small right now,
nurture it with your words as you would
a tiny seedling in unyielding ground.

You bless your husband or wife when you declare the good you see in his or her life. When you verify someone's good character with your words, it can't help but build up more character—kindness, generosity, patience, truthfulness, compassion, and moral purity. Even if the good you see in your spouse seems infinitesimally small right now, nurture it with your words as you would a tiny seedling in unyielding ground.

In the summer of 2011 I went through a battle against breast cancer—or I should say, my husband and I went through it together. I was not alone. With each doctor's appointment, hospital visit, bone scan, and blood test, during the second opinion and the third, Ken was my strongest advocate. And in my weakest moments when I felt as though the ravages of chemotherapy would overwhelm me, he buoyed me up with words of affirmation: "Joni, I'm really impressed with your valor . . . what with your chronic pain and quadriplegia, and now this cancer. I've never seen anyone face cancer treatment so bravely!" His words poured more courage into my heart. What's more, they pointed me to the source of that courage: Christ Himself. (Author and educator Sam Crabtree has more to say about this in his excellent little book *Practicing Affirmation.*)

First Corinthians 14:12 says, "So it is with you. Since you are eager to have spiritual gifts, try to excel in gifts that build up the church." Words of affirmation are to marriage what Miracle-Gro is to your flower bed. Good things *have* to blossom! Most of us know better than to talk down to others, and that principle is even more important in marriage where most words go right under the magnifying glass. Words that point out a Christ-like characteristic in your spouse grow confidence and trust—and the Bible tells us to excel in the art of building up those we love (1 Corinthians 14:12).

Additionally, affirming Christ-like characteristics gives you a solid position from which you can offer honest criticisms. During my twelve-month battle against cancer, my confidence and trust in my husband grew leaps and bounds— and so now, when he offers words of criticism or correction, I listen. He's gained the right to be heard. His encouraging words give him a platform from which to say things that would have splintered our relationship in the beginning of our marriage.

No one trusts a person who constantly doles out disapproval and denigration. But if you have poured true Christian encouragement into your spouse, his or her faith in you grows. Your spouse sees that you genuinely care, that you do try to see the best in him or her.

WHAT ARE SOME EFFECTIVE WAYS TO BLESS YOUR MATE?

When your husband is working on a series of projects around the house, commend him for the good work he's done on one task before he moves on to the next. Say, for instance, "I love the way you pay attention to details. The primer you put on before that paint job made the finished product look so much nicer!"

Explain to your wife that her example inspired you to take some good action with the family, around the home, or in the neighborhood. Tell her, for instance, "I decided to get the kids Baskin-Robbins gift certificates because I see how much they appreciate it when *you* do extra little things like that."

Loan your spouse something of value. When you place a personal treasure in the hands of another, it's a signal to that person that you recognize good character traits that elevate your confidence in his or her trustworthiness.

Write a note of encouragement and tuck it in her purse or mail it to his office. In it, affirm some of the Christian virtues you see in your spouse, virtues that your words will strengthen.

Think of specific ways you can excel in
building up your husband or wife today.

Oh, what life-giving power can be found in an encouraging word! So think of specific ways you can excel in building up your husband or wife today, especially if he or she is struggling with health or job issues or coping with pain. Proverbs 12:25 says, "An anxious heart weighs a man down, but a kind word cheers him up."

Friend, your good words can gladden the hearts of the most important people in your life today. Your words not only touch one's spirit, but they can also actually *change* that person's countenance. (Your affirmation may not, however, change his mind about taking out the garbage, but that's okay. Some molehills are not worth dying on.) So whether you send an e-mail, tell your spouse in person, write a letter, talk over the phone, or write a quick note, remember that what you say today has the capacity to transform the countenance and the character of the most important person in your life.

1. These insights on affirmation are gleaned from Sam Crabtree, *Practicing Affirmation: God-Centered Praise of Those Who Are Not God* (Wheaton, IL: Crossway, 2011).

Joni Eareckson Tada and her team at the Joni and Friends International Disability Center are dedicated to sharing Christ's love with special-needs families around the world. Joni and her husband, Ken, reside in Agoura Hills, California, and she says proudly, "I love it whenever Ken, a top fly fisherman, snags the big trout!"

10

Ask Older Couples What Works for Them

Bill and Pam Farrel

When we got married, we knew we loved God and we knew we loved each other, but we had far more questions about successful marriage than answers. Neither of us wanted to model our marriage after our parents' marriages, so we went looking for advice.

We used to stand in the back of the church until most people were seated. We would then look for couples who appeared to have been married awhile yet still liked each other. A couple that was laughing together or making affectionate physical contact was an obvious draw for us. We would then sit right behind a couple like that, and during the greeting time I (Bill) would look at the husband and ask, "You two look like you are in love. Is this real?"

Every time the couple looked at each other and said, "Yes, it is," I would then ask, "How did you do it?" The usual response was "We don't have time to talk about that right now, but if you want to have lunch after church, we can discuss it."

This was very helpful to us for two reasons. First, we were a young married couple on a tight budget, so it was great to be taken out to lunch! More important, though, we got real advice from real people. These couples knew more than they realized as they shared with us the practical insights they had acquired over the years.

What follows is some of the best advice we received from these couples.

WOMEN BUILD TRUST BY CONNECTING

I (Bill) am constantly amazed at Pam's need to connect verbally. Sometimes her conversations have a main point, and sometimes they are like random walks in the neighborhood, but they are always important to her. I can't tell from her tone of voice whether she is facing an issue she needs to solve or telling me about the competitors on the latest reality TV show because she is capable of the same level of enthusiasm for both. When I was encouraged to listen with curiosity, I discovered a powerful way to help her feel valued, and that makes our relationship work more smoothly.

If I want my wife to trust me, I need to develop the ability to be intrigued with her conversations.

When I neglect this need, it seems as if every conversation is a potential starting point for the next argument. From my male perspective, I wish marriage could be more efficient, but that's just not the way it works. If I want my wife to trust me, I need to develop the ability to be intrigued with her conversations.

MEN BUILD TRUST THROUGH SUCCESS

Just as I (Pam) need to be listened to, it is just as important to Bill that he feel capable and strong. Initially, that quality presented something of a puzzle to me, because I am acutely aware of my own shortcomings. I have always lived by the motto "I might as well point out my flaws before anyone else does. That way we can laugh about them more." I assumed Bill probably had that same attitude, even though one of our lunchtime mentors told me to never deliberately embarrass my husband in public.

My first exposure to Bill's need to feel successful happened early in our relationship. We were dancing romantically at a gathering of friends. Bill dipped me in a final crescendo and then dropped me on the ground and started backing away. I got up and asked him what happened. He whispered, "I just ripped my pants."

He said it so low, I asked, "What did you say?"

He repeated himself, "I just ripped my pants. We need to go."

Well, I thought it was funny, so I turned him around and shouted out to everyone else in the room, "Look! Bill just ripped his pants!" I laughed. Everyone else in the room laughed. Bill, however, did something very different. He grew angry and silent. Very angry and very silent.

At that point I understood the wisdom of the advice I received and how important it is for me to heed it. When I help Bill feel successful in conversation, in his career, in our romance, in our lovemaking, and in our decisions, his sense of well-being soars, and he is easy to live with. When I ignore this need and get too critical with him, he grows silent and uncooperative. I keep reminding myself that it is my job to cheer Bill on, and it is God's job to change him.

It was comforting when we were told that conflict is to be expected.

CONFLICT IS NORMAL EVEN FOR LOVING COUPLES

We both grew up in homes with lots of yelling and destructive arguments. When we got married, we decided we wouldn't argue much because we were deeply in love and committed to open, honest, and direct communication. Well, it turns out we're pretty normal: we have had some pretty intense disagreements. It was comforting when we were told that such conflict is to be expected. In fact, there are a number of good reasons why healthy, loving couples argue:

We argue because we are intimate

No one knows me (Bill) like Pam does. She spends more time with me, more money with me, and more effort trying to figure me out than anyone else I know. As a result, she encourages me greatly—and she finds the hot buttons in my soul. If there is a fear in me, she will pick up on it. If there is an immature reaction in me, she will notice it. When she comments on the good stuff she sees in me, I praise her. But when she finds the wounds, I want to push her away, and that's when the arguments begin.

Conversely, no one knows me (Pam) like Bill, and his opinion goes straight to my heart—for good or bad—faster than anyone else's.

We argue because we disagree

We are both strong, thinking, opinionated adults. We know what we like, what we want, and what we believe to be true. When we agree, it's nothing short of awesome. When we disagree, both of us are usually stubborn about our position.

Our longest argument lasted for a year. We disagreed on how much time Pam should invest in her education and ministry while our kids were young, and we had a hard time moving off our positions to some common ground in the middle. We would talk at length, run out of time, pray for each other, and reschedule the argument. The prayer and rescheduling increased our commitment to each other while we wrestled with the issue we couldn't resolve. We eventually saw eye to eye on a schedule, and I (Bill) adopted an attitude toward Pam's drive that helped me see it as healthy for our family.

We argue because we love each other

This insight was the most revealing one for us, and it makes sense. Because we love each other, no one has the same influence on us that we have on each other. That's why a brief glance can completely change the atmosphere of our home. A single mutter can ruin an otherwise good day, while a flirtatious comment can rescue a dreary one. Pam's body language and tone of voice are like water to me (Bill): I either float on the buoyancy they provide or drown in the ensuing flood of hurt and even anger.

In the same way, Bill's words are like gourmet food to me (Pam). His loving words fill me up like a grand buffet, but when he gives me the silent treatment, I feel as if I am starving. Nobody else on earth has this kind of effect on us. We love each other deeply, so everything we do and say has a profound impact on the other. Hence sometimes our love for each other gives rise to "intense fellowship."

Couples don't fall out of love. They
fall out of forgiveness.

Forgive quickly

We were told emphatically that marriage is a relationship of two imperfect people who need to forgive each other often.

One couple even said, "Couples don't fall out of love. They fall out of forgiveness." Case in point: When I (Bill) lost five thousand dollars of Pam's inheritance on a bad investment, I was really glad we had been challenged to learn the art of forgiveness.

THREE IS BETTER THAN TWO

Early on in our marriage, we believed we had enough love and enough smarts to have a solid relationship in our own power. Over time, however, we have clung to the advice that Jesus is the best support our relationship could have. The most memorable moments in our life together have been those times when one of us had a thought that we knew was a gift from the Holy Spirit. I (Bill), for instance, will never forget the day Pam handed me a list of places we have made love as I was walking to the front of the church to preach. I thought she was handing me an announcement to read to the congregation. Nope, she was just flirting with the pastor.

I (Pam) will never forget the time Bill was running through our house to pick up his briefcase. He couldn't stay long, but he stopped to say, "Pam, I wish I was independently wealthy and could stay home and love you all day long, but I have to go." Neither of us is smart enough to come up with those kinds of ideas on our own, and we are extremely grateful that the Holy Spirit feeds us great moments.

ETERNAL IMPACT

The couples who bought us lunch in those early days of our marriage didn't realize they were mentoring us, but our lives were forever changed because they fed us. The wisdom they shared were seeds for thought that eventually turned into books like *Men Are Like Waffles, Women Are Like Spaghetti* and *Red-Hot Monogamy*. Those books are helping thousands of couples all around the globe.

If you are new to marriage, seek out the wisdom of those with years of joyful experience under their belt. And if you, by God's grace, have found something that works well for your marriage, take a young couple to lunch. You never know where the little bit of advice about marriage you plant may blossom into marriage-saving hope and guidance for that couple.

Bill and Pam Farrel are international relationship specialists. They have penned more than thirty-five books, including Men Are Like Waffles—Women Are Like Spaghetti *and* The 10 Best Decisions Every Parent Can Make. *Pam is coauthor of* Raising a Modern-Day Princess, Becoming a Modern-Day Princess, *and* LOL with God. *More relationship resources for marriage and family are available at their website, www.Love-Wise.com.*

11

Nine Words That Have Helped Us Stay Married

Bob Waliszewski

Don't ever threaten your spouse with divorce[1] or separation."[2]

Without question, these nine words comprise the single best bit of marriage advice I was ever given. Although I'd love to give credit where credit's due, I simply can't remember where I heard it. But I can speak to the impact that these words to the wise have had on Leesa and me.

Leesa and I intentionally discussed this principle before we got married. At that point in our relationship (when everything was roses, waterfalls, and butterflies), it probably seemed as unnecessary as if we'd bandied about how we might handle the potential pitfalls of living in the White House. Still, we agreed that we would *never, ever* in any situation resort to saying things like this:

1. If you don't like it, just leave.
2. You never listen to me. You never see things my way. I can't take this anymore. I'm out of here!
3. Let me put it to you this way: You're either going to change, or I'm walking out of this relationship. I will not argue with you about this anymore. It's your decision. Do you want me to stay or not?
4. You have aggravated me to the point of no return. Although I said I'd never threaten divorce, I had no way of knowing you'd be like this. I've got to protect my own sanity!
5. I know the Bible says that unfaithfulness is the only reason for divorce. However, I'm sure the Lord would understand if I left you due to the fact that you're always (fill in the blank here with such things as "nagging me," "complaining about the way I do things," "disrespecting me," etc.).

FAILED EXPECTATIONS

As I look back over our thirty-three years together, our fights have been relatively rare. Sadly, though, many have been doozies, sparked by some of the dumbest things. For us, these blowups are often linked to failed expectations or the different ways we view or handle things.

As an example of failed expectations, I'll air some of my dirty laundry. I'm a runner, and I used to train for marathons. While I could handle the ten- and twelve-mile training runs, once I got up into the fifteen-, eighteen-, and twenty-mile range, my body was spent. All I wanted to do after logging my miles was hang out on the sofa.

Meanwhile, Leesa was expecting that I would be part of the family and go bike riding or hiking. It's not that I refused to do these things, but I was often self-centered. I had plenty of reasons to justify my loafing. I had, after all, just spent two to three hours on the trail. But Leesa was right: I had children at home who needed my attention. Life shouldn't revolve around me. During these times, however, I often didn't see the situation as rationally as I do now. My expectation was simple: I needed rest. Leesa's expectation was also simple: I needed to join the family. These unmet expectations mixed like oil and water.

DIFFERING VIEWPOINTS

In addition to having expectations that sometimes conflict, Leesa and I also often view things differently. To say that about a married couple is like saying the sky is blue. We *all* have times when we view things differently. Leesa and I have a version of the proverbial toothpaste-tube squeezing dilemma, but ours centers on bottled water.

Here's how it works: I have this self-made rule that water should, for the most part, be free. I drink tap water, which in my part of Colorado is clean and tasty. That said, I'm okay with buying the occasional case of bottled water, but once purchased, I use those individual bottles sparingly due to their cost. Once I open a bottle of water, I cannot waste the contents. Plus, I must drink it all and consume the contents within about thirty minutes of unscrewing the plastic cap.

Leesa, on the other hand, has no problem with leaving a half-dozen containers of bottled water in her car, all at various fluid levels. Her belief is that drinking water is so healthy that the simple act of taking in any H_2O far outweighs the cost of the bottles. What's more, she disdains public drinking fountains due to their germ factor. And she's not crazy about drinking "old" water either. To her, if she ends up throwing a bunch of unfinished water bottles in the trash, it's still money well spent.

Eventually, we've come to realize that we'll never see eye to eye on the water-bottle issue. *And you know, that's okay.* I will continue to down that rare bottle of water in a half hour. And I'll hold my tongue when I hop in her car and have to move four or five partially finished containers just to sit down. (Okay, I admit: that's still hard for me!) But I've come to realize that water bottles are just not worth arguing over.

I'm sure you and your spouse lock horns over "little" things too. Keep in mind that all loving couples disagree. And, from time to time, all committed couples have to deal with doozy-big blowups. But it's how we handle ourselves in the midst of the battle that leads either toward healing or irreparable fallout.

THE MARITAL PRESET BUTTON

When we're angry and feeling hurt and disrespected, that is not the time for us to try to establish rock-solid boundaries that will guide us through the storm. We need to know where those guardrails are ahead of time. That's why Leesa and I established our guardrails before we were married— we *preset* these guidelines—that we would not add fuel to the fires of our anger by bringing the word *divorce* into the verbal mix. We also agreed that we wouldn't leave in the middle of a fight.

Now let me define *leave* here. It's okay for two contentious partners to take a time-out and give each other space. They may find that space in their own home, but sometimes one might want to take a walk, get control over his or her emotions, and come back at a later time to work through the issue. That kind of space is healthy enough, but Leesa and I have never allowed each other to run home to parents, go to a hotel, or find a friend who would have a more sympathetic ear.

Although self-imposed, those guidelines are tough to follow in times of anger and hurt when feelings of betrayal and disrespect dominate. During those times, we want to seek out someone who will side with us, who will make us feel that we were right and our partner was wrong. But finding someone to side with us doesn't bring us any closer to reconciliation and healing in our relationship. In fact, it most likely takes us further away from reconciling and keeps us away longer.

WHAT WORKED FOR US

Here's how Leesa and I have successfully worked through our arguments. Since we clearly were and still are committed to never divorcing, we never threatened it. And that left us only one option: *working out our problems.* We had pledged before we got married that we wouldn't use the threat of divorce or separation as a weapon, and we have stayed true to that.

In times of anger, I find an overwhelming sense of comfort in knowing—even in the midst of the storm—that I can count on Leesa to remain with me. And I know she feels the same way. Sure, at times she's convinced she married the biggest jerk on the planet. But she also knows that the jerk she married will be there in the morning, and the next day, and the next week, and the next decade.

I'm convinced that relationships that don't have the true spirit of "till death do us part" are unstable relationships. Who knows how many couples have split up simply because one partner wanted to beat the other to the knockout punch of packing the bags and walking out the door?

But just because Leesa and I established this "don't threaten divorce" boundary in our lives doesn't mean we haven't still thought about it a time or two. It also doesn't mean I haven't been tempted to ignore this boundary and threaten divorce anyway. I know Leesa has too. But we've stayed the course: we have not gone against our better judgment and intimidated our spouse by spewing those menacing words. Having divorce off the table helps simplify the healing process, which isn't to say that it makes it easy. Just easier.

*Having divorce off the table helps simplify
the healing process, which isn't to say
that it makes it easy. Just easier.*

MR. RIGHT ISN'T ALWAYS RIGHT

Like a lot of men in an argument, I tend to posture as if I'm always right. I think that if I just restate my viewpoint, say it in a louder tone, roll my eyes just the right way, or point out the fallacies of Leesa's take on the situation, I will win her over. Then peace will reign in the home once again. Of course, it never works that way. But when skirmishes occur, those are my fallback positions. I admit my natural tenden cies are bad enough, but imagine how much worse it would be if one of my verbal weapons was to bully Leesa with the threat of leaving her.

Every once in a while, though, I get it right. I'm able to head off what could be a heated squabble by doing the following:

1. Listening—*really* listening—to Leesa's view.
2. Speaking her view back to her using words such as "What I hear you saying is＿＿＿＿＿＿＿."

3. Asking Leesa her opinion about what would solve the conflict.

4. Denying myself for the sake of our marriage and showing some true humility by backing down (Yes, that's very hard to do!).

5. Apologizing—not for having an opinion, but for the way I handled myself.

6. Not keeping score of who did what, who compromised, and who made the effort to reconcile. If anything, situations work out much better in the long run when I race to be the first person to settle things.

7. Avoiding the silent treatment. If I need some time to cool off, I do so with a full explanation. ("Honey, I'm gonna walk around the block a couple of times to clear my head and think more about what we've been arguing about. I'll be back in thirty minutes.")

8. Steering clear of using the words *always* and *never*, and not saying demeaning things during a fight, such as "You *never* say anything nice about me to your parents." "You *always* act so immature when you're around your high school buddies." "I do everything for the kids because you're a self-centered, egotistical slob who *never* thinks of anyone but him/herself." A better way to express the latter would be "Help me understand why you failed to pick Billy up at school today and what you plan to do so that it doesn't happen again. I know you care about our children, but we both know we can't be getting any more calls like this from the principal."

9. At times the best thing a couple can do when they're fighting is to go out in public. You'll find that you don't raise your voice, and your demeanor will be more civil and Christlike.

TILL DEATH DO US PART

Leesa and I are individuals who—although extremely committed to and deeply in love with each other—see life, people, situations, and opportunities differently.

The lion's share of the time, we tackle our disagreements quite civilly and respectfully. Sometimes it takes awhile for us to reach a compromise, but we do get there. Every now and again we slip up and get significantly irked with each other, and for a moment, we see the person we married as a broomstick-riding bonehead.

Since divorce is not at all an option, it's nice to know we will get beyond this fallacious imagery. We know that instead of threatening to take off our wedding rings, we'll be working to respectfully and lovingly get beyond our disagreements.

Whether you're just starting out on this journey we call marriage or have been married sixty years, it's never too late to implement these nine important words: "Don't ever threaten your spouse with divorce or separation."

In the years since we said our vows, we've had our share of ups and downs. We've had our share of disagreements. We've had our share of blowups. But looking back and looking forward, we meant our vows when we first spoke them, and we still mean them today: we're in this thing "till death do us part."

1. Leesa and I agree with Focus on the Family's policy on divorce, dating, and remarriage. Focus holds that divorce and remarriage are biblically justified in three instances: unrepentant sexual immorality, permanent abandonment by an unbelieving spouse, or when the divorce took place prior to salvation. When addressing the issue of dating and potential remarriage, it is incumbent upon us to point to Scripture's guidance and encourage individuals in this situation to seek counsel from their pastor and/or a Christian counselor.

2. We do believe that separation is necessary in the case of physical abuse. If physical abuse is taking place in your marriage, the first concern is safety. If you are being physically abused or threatened, get to a safe place. Don't remain in a situation where you are likely to be hurt again. Contact your local abuse hotline or the police. Though you may think what is occurring is justified and you don't have any options, don't believe those lies. Physical abuse is never justified or normal, and there are always options and people who can help you.

Bob Waliszewski is a parent and former youth pastor. He's also the director of Plugged In® Online, *which is visited about one million times each month by people looking for detailed, trustworthy information about today's entertainment. He has two grown children. Bob and Leesa make their home in Colorado.*

12

Grow as a Couple and as Individuals

Frank Pastore

In the late 1980s my wife, Gina, and I decided to go on staff with Campus Crusade for Christ (now called Cru). We thought, *Okay, together we'll probably make thirty or forty or fifty thousand dollars a year, and we'll just do ministry.* Then we found out we had to raise support. We'd had no clue we'd have to do that! Formerly, I'd been a Major League baseball pitcher making a nice salary. Now we'd have to go around to couples saying, "Will you support us for fifty dollars a month?"

That was a very humbling and odd experience. But we managed to raise some support, and I was invited to meet with Dr. Bill Bright at Arrowhead Springs in San Bernardino, California, which was the headquarters of Campus Crusade before it moved to Florida.

IT'S ALL ABOUT ME

Dr. Bright explicitly asked Gina to come along. In my head it was *I'm going to meet with Dr. Bill Bright, and I'm going to go on the staff of Campus Crusade, and God's calling me to ministry, and, oh yeah, Gina's coming too.* I was so unbelievably arrogant and me-focused. My attitude was *I'm going to be so spiritual and go on staff.* That's often the attitude of a guy who comes to Christ before his wife, a guy who thinks he's smart.

Well, Gina and I arrived at the headquarters in Arrowhead Springs. Because they were still deciding whether they were going to take me on staff, I was all prepped to do this wonderfully impressive "Gee, look how smart and spiritual I am" kind of thing with Dr. Bright. Of course, in hindsight, I had no clue what was going on, and I was in for a surprise.

After we spent a few minutes in the waiting room, the receptionist said, "Dr. Bright will see you now" and ushered us into his office. We exchanged pleasantries: "Hello, Dr. Bright. Nice to meet you. This is my wife, Gina" and so on. Within moments, maybe three minutes tops, the pleasantries were done. Now it was time to talk.

WINDING UP FOR THE PITCH

I was all ready to tell Dr. Bright about the books I'd read and how the Lord was leading me and all this pseudospiritual stuff. I couldn't wait to wow him. But as I was winding up for my pitch, he very politely and elegantly held up his palm as if to say, "No. Hold on." Then he turned his whole body toward Gina and talked with her for the next half hour. I barely got a word in! It was very clear he was talking to Gina exclusively, and the first thought that crossed my mind was, *Oh. He doesn't think she can cut it. He's concerned that she's not ready for ministry.*

Dr. Bright asked Gina all the questions like "How're the kids?" and "How'd you grow up?" and "When did you meet the Lord?" and that kind of stuff. Then, after just *thirty-five* minutes, he had heard enough, and the meeting was done.

The phrase I would use to describe Dr. Bright would be *thundering humility.* He was just wonderful. But I didn't understand that at the time. In fact, I left thinking, *I didn't get a chance to do all my stuff!* I'd prepped like crazy. I had all of these notes. I was going to be so impressive. I had no clue what had just happened, and I wondered why it had happened this way — why he had talked only to my wife and not to me. I didn't want to tell Gina, "Well, it was obviously because he doesn't think you're spiritual enough to be on the Campus Crusade staff like me."

GETTING MY COMEUPPANCE

Shortly after the meeting with Dr. Bright, I called Wendel Deyo, national director of Athletes in Action. He was the guy who led me to the Lord, and I wanted to let him know how the meeting had gone.

While I was talking to Wendel on the phone, he said, "Oh, there was a lot more to that. No, it wasn't about checking to see if Gina was ready. There's more to the story, but I'll tell you when you get here."

When I met with Wendel man-to-man, he very politely raked me over the coals and basically said, "Even though he was talking to Gina, it was all about you because the measure of a man's ministry is how he treats his wife and his children. Men can con men all the time because we think it's about externals and performance. It's not. The measure of a man's ministry is the spiritual health of his wife and his children." That insight—that implicit advice—began to shape my life for the better.

That was an important and humbling lesson, one that has proved true over the years since then. And even though I didn't get a chance to wow Dr. Bright, we were invited to be on staff with CCC. We served there for two years, until I went to seminary at Talbot School of Theology.

YOU ARE NOT INDEPENDENT OF YOUR SPOUSE

That story illustrates a key point for couples: God may be calling one of you into ministry or a career, and you may have the gifting, but unless you work together as a couple, you're going to struggle.

You have to realize that when God calls you, He has an equally important purpose for your spouse; His call to you is not to be independent of your spouse. So if God is prompting one of you to move in a certain direction, you've got to ask yourselves and Him, "How does this work for us together?" Unless you're on the same page, it may not be the right thing to do.

You have to realize that when God calls
you, He has an equally important purpose
for your spouse; His call to you is not
to be independent of your spouse.

Most couples over the centuries married really young, but that's not the case today. People aren't getting married too early. In fact, now they're getting married too late. The challenge today is that couples may have developed too strong a sense of self and not know how to meld together as a couple. They may not know how to compromise. They've lived on their own, they've had an apartment or a house, they've been paying bills, building a career, all that. Then, of course, it complicates things when couples live together before marriage. So our advice to couples is, find out how your careers, your ministry, and your interests can work together.

DEVELOPING YOUR IDENTITIES

While you have to work together and grow as a couple, both of you also have to grow as individuals. You see, you are two individuals joining together to create this third thing, the couple. But if you don't have a strong sense of yourself as an individual, then suddenly the other person and the couple become all-important. If you don't nourish yourself, then you begin to lose yourself, and of course you rebel against that. Just because you got married doesn't mean you suddenly lose your identity. You're still who you are, and you bring that into the marriage.

Gina and I struggled with identity early in our marriage. We are an anomaly because we married so young (Gina was sixteen and I was twenty-one), and we had not yet developed a strong sense of self. Gina had even quit high school to get married. By the time I left my baseball career, I was twenty-nine and Gina was twenty-five. Both our identities had gotten wrapped up in the baseball thing, but it was over. Who were we now?

Gina got her sense of self primarily through her role as a wife and mother, and that got a little harmful, toxic, and counterproductive. We were going to a church in our hometown of Upland, California, and the women's director, Edna Myers, took Gina aside and said, "You really need to grow as an individual and find out who Gina is and what her gifts are." This was really key for the Lord to speak through Edna and give Gina that advice because it had a tremendously positive effect on our marriage.

At that point Gina began to grow as a person. We had two small children, so she didn't have a lot of time to go back to school or anything like that, but based on Edna's advice, she decided to get her high school diploma. That was very scary for her. She felt like she'd been out of school a long time and wouldn't be able to pass the GED. But she passed and then enrolled in a community college where she majored in business management. That's when she really started to find herself. She also went for counseling. Meanwhile, I was trying to find my identity now that I was no longer a Major League Baseball pitcher. Since the age of five, I'd grown up answering the question, "Frankie, what are you going to be when you grow up?" with "I'm going to be a baseball player." And, like most males, my identity was completely wrapped up in what I did instead of who I was.

After my career came to an end, I got a lot of my identity and defined myself in terms of being married to Gina. So the issue became "Who am I as a husband? What does that mean about who I am as a father?" Because these roles had never been modeled for me, I didn't know the answers. I had grown up in a very unstable environment with a sociopathic mother and an emotionally detached father. I had spent years trying to unravel my mother's lies and separate truth from fiction, but I was still very confused. Eventually I went to counseling and began to figure out who I was. That was a hard process but so important to helping me integrate the pieces of my personality.

YOU NEED FRIENDS

Through the years, another thing that has helped us grow both as a couple and as individuals has been friendship. If your spouse is your only friend, you're going to place heavy expectations on him or her to meet all your needs, and that becomes toxic. You need other people to enrich your lives.

To grow as individuals, you need individual playmates. Their spouses don't need to be friends with your spouse. Gina, for example, encourages me to take motorcycle trips, so that's my playtime, my time to hang out with my friends. Likewise, Gina goes places with her female friends who are not the wives of my motorcycle buddies.

To grow in your marriage, you need married friends where both husband and wife get along with both husband and wife. If I like him and Gina likes her, it's perfect. We can vacation together, we can play together, and we end up becoming very close, lifelong friends. You have to be strategic about this, though. You have only so many vacation days per year and only so much free time, especially when you have kids. You have only so many Friday or Saturday nights when you can get a sitter and go out as a couple. There's time for only so many friendships.

It sounds sort of cold and analytical, but again, time is finite, and we have to make hard decisions. If you let everyone in, pretty soon you don't have any time alone as a couple, and on top of that, your friendships are going nowhere. Why? Because you're always connecting at the surface level; you never go deep. We all need couples who are close, intimate friends—couples we want to spend our lives with.

MAKE SURE YOU'RE PLAYING ON THE SAME TEAM

Finally, marriage comes down to teamwork—to working and making decisions together as a couple in order to accomplish what's best for the marriage and the family. Gina is the hub around which everything in our family operates. I'm the spiritual head, technically, but the way it operationally works out, she's the one who sustains a lot of the relationships with our friends and our kids because my job as a radio talk-show host is an all-consuming kind of thing. There's no way I could do my show without Gina. I don't see how people face the demands of a career without a good marriage and an incredibly supportive spouse.

Marriage comes down to teamwork—to
working and making decisions together
as a couple in order to accomplish what's
best for the marriage and the family.

When I refer to Gina as my Wife, that's with a capital W. So much time, energy, effort, thought, prayer, and love goes into that role. She's not merely my spouse; she's my best friend, my primary counselor, my go-to person in matters both professional and personal. People may see me and hear my name all the time, but anyone who knows us is well aware that Gina's behind the whole thing. Together we are an incredible team.

And—if I do say so myself—I've grown a lot since the day Dr. Bright interviewed that pridefully arrogant and stupid guy who thought it was all about me.

Frank Pastore is the host of the most-listened-to live Christian talk show in the country on 99.5 KKLA. Frank and his wife, Gina, have been married for thirty-four years, and they have two adult children and one grandson. For seven years, Frank pitched in the big leagues with the Cincinnati Reds and Minnesota Twins before attending Tulbot Seminary. Later he earned another master's in political philosophy at Claremont Graduate University. Frank and Gina live near Los Angeles.

13

Putting Sex on the Calendar

Jill Savage

M ark and I describe ourselves as being married twenty-
eight years . . . eighteen of them happily. We've had
some difficult seasons and have found marriage counseling to be an important strategy for getting and keeping our
marriage on track. Some of the best marriage advice I ever
received came from a marriage counselor, and whenever we
learn a valuable strategy, we are quick to share it with others. So here it is, and this particular piece of advice is about
the importance of scheduling sex.

One afternoon my phone rang, and the young mom on
the other end of the phone poured out her frustrations. She
desired sex, but her husband could not care less. As the parents of five, all under the age of six, they rarely found time
for each other outside the bedroom, let alone inside. She
confessed that she felt they were more like roommates than
lovers.

I listened with understanding. As the mother of five myself, I know the struggle of keeping a family marriage-centered, not child-centered. I know the difficulty of finding time for just the two of us. And I know the challenge of differing sexual drives.

When she finally paused to catch her breath, I explained some of the strategies Mark and I found to keep our marriage a priority. This mom and I talked about creative date ideas, inexpensive childcare options, and the importance of connecting on a daily basis. I asked her if she and her husband ever considered scheduling their sex life. She responded with an awkward silence.

Finally, she laughed and said, "You're kidding, right? Sex is supposed to be spontaneous. Nobody *schedules* sex."

PENCIL IT IN—IN CODE!

Throughout our marriage, Mark and I have been at opposite ends of the spectrum when it comes to our sex drives. Mark thinks about sex once every seventeen seconds. I think about it once every seventeen days. And this wasn't our only marital challenge.

Our differing sex drives was just one issue among many in our hurting relationship. During a healing season of counseling though, we learned some new strategies for communication, conflict resolution, and compromise concerning our sexual differences. That's also when we first discovered the concept of scheduling sex.

At first, just like that young mom, we couldn't get past the misconception that sex isn't something to be scheduled. Who says sex should always be spontaneous? Movies, TV shows, magazine articles, and romance novels, that's who!

If we're not careful, we begin to use the media to determine what's "right" or "normal." If we do, then we're using the wrong measuring stick. We can't allow our culture or the media to set the direction for our relationship. Instead, we need to apply our God-given creativity to find the time and set the strategies to make our sex life within our marriage work.

If we're not careful, we begin to use the media to determine what's "right" or "normal."

Once Mark and I were able to accept that scheduling sex wasn't such a crazy idea, we put it into place within our marriage. Today, we're still amazed at the practice that has transformed our physical relationship.

How does planned lovemaking benefit a marriage? Consider these advantages.

IT ELIMINATES "THE ASK"

In most marriages, one partner possesses a higher desire than the other and requests sex more often, while his or her partner rarely asks for physical intimacy. For the spouse with a higher desire, the fear of rejection often sets in. One becomes weary of regularly having to ask, or even beg, for sex.

When a couple can agree on a basic schedule for sex, it takes the guesswork out. Of course there is still room for occasional spontaneity, but the calendar reassures the higher-sex-drive mate that it will happen, and not only that—they know *when*! Usually the frequency is less often than the partner with a higher desire would want and more often than the partner with a lesser desire may want. They are meeting on middle ground.

IT INCREASES DESIRE

For the partner with a diminished desire, scheduling sex engages the brain, which is the largest sex organ in the human body. The brain needs to be clued in to prepare the body for a sexual response. Most people who have a lower sexual drive simply don't think about sex very often. Scheduling jump-starts this process.

Scheduling sex engages the brain, which is the largest sex organ in the human body.

Once sex is on the calendar, it serves as a reminder to think about sex, prepares us mentally for being together physically, and primes us to get in the mood. When I complained to a friend about having trouble getting in the mood, she said, "Jill, you're trying to go from making meatloaf to making love in thirty seconds flat. You can't do that. You have to have a strategy for getting from point A to point B."

Rarely does the partner with an increased desire need to get in the mood, but the partner with a lesser desire may need to work at it. When sex is on the calendar, it serves as a prompt to set strategies in motion. Scheduling sex reminds spouses that they're working together toward the goal of intimacy, valuing their appointed rendezvous, and doing whatever it takes to make it happen.

IT INCREASES ANTICIPATION

When lovemaking is kept on the front burner, anticipation builds. Both husband and wife begin to prepare for their marital recreation.

Have you ever thought of sex as recreation? It is! God gave us the gift of sex as a form of recreation in our marriage. It's our own private playground where God intends for us to enjoy physical pleasure.

When sex is on the schedule, we enjoy planning our time together, because we both have the same goal. We can even become lifelong learners in the art of giving pleasure to each other. Keeping a couple of Christian sexual technique books on the shelf may help us develop into experts in giving physical pleasure to each other. This simple act of scheduling sex builds anticipation and fosters an opportunity to learn and excel at loving our spouse.

IT ALLOWS FOR PRIME-TIME PLANNING

He prefers nighttime when he can be romantic. She prefers daytime when she's not so tired. They decide to put lovemaking on their calendar twice a week: Tuesday at noon (he comes home for lunch and she arranges a sitter for the kids) and Friday at night (after a warm bath and an evening of watching a movie together or going out on a date). This schedule worked well for one couple we mentored.

Most couples not only differ in their desires concerning frequency of sex, but also in their ideas about what atmosphere is conducive to sex. Some people struggle with making love anytime the children are in the vicinity. Others prefer a certain time of the day. When you put your lovemaking on the calendar, you can work to accommodate those likes and dislikes to meet the desires of both.

*When you put your lovemaking on the calendar,
you can work to accommodate the likes and
dislikes of each partner to meet the desires of both.*

IT HELPS COUPLES PREPARE PHYSICALLY

I used to tease my husband that once we got on a lovemaking schedule, it sure took the pressure off shaving my legs every day! On the serious side, there's value in preparing yourself physically to make love to your mate. A hot bath or shower, a freshly shaved body, and some great-smelling lotion often relax us for physical intimacy. It also builds anticipation as you prepare to be with your spouse.

If weariness keeps you from being excited about sex, an early evening nap may be just the key if lovemaking is on the agenda that night. Since some of the guesswork is out of the mix, we can prepare not only mentally, but physically.

IT BUILDS TRUST

If we're going to commit to lovemaking on a regular basis, we need to honor our word and agreement. Honoring our word builds trust and deepens intimacy. On the rare occasion that something prevents the regularly scheduled lovemaking, spouses need to communicate their value of sexual intimacy so they can make alternate plans to meet those physical and emotional needs. This kind of communication is key to successful intimacy.

Several weeks after that initial conversation, I spoke again with that young mom. Her voice held an enthusiasm I hadn't heard before. I asked her how things were going, and she said that she and her husband were working on some new ways to energize and invest in their marriage.

She concluded by saying, "Now don't bother calling Friday around noon, because no one is going to answer the phone!" I knew that she had learned the same secret we had learned years ago. While spontaneous sex may have its place in life, scheduling sex always has its place on our calendar!

Featured on Focus on the Family and Crosswalk.com and serving as the host of the Heartbeat *radio program, Jill Savage is the founder and director of Hearts at Home, an organization that encourages moms. Jill and her husband, Mark, have five children—three who are married—and two grandchildren. They make their home in Normal, Illinois. Jill is an author and speaker who is passionate about encouraging families. She is also the author of seven books including* Professionalizing Motherhood, My Heart's at Home, Real Moms . . . Real Jesus, *and her most recent release, coauthored with her husband,* Living with Less So Your Family Has More. *For more information, visit www.jillsavage.org.*

14

Attitude Is a Choice

Stormie Omartian

I love it when the Lord speaks to my heart specifically regarding something I've been concerned about for a long time. It's like cool refreshing water being poured over my weary soul that has been in a hot, dry desert of despair for far too long.

One of the best pieces of advice I ever received on marriage came directly from God when I was praying to Him about something my husband, Michael, had done that upset me. Not only did I know his decision was wrong, but I knew it would probably affect me for the rest of my life. No, it wasn't the Big A. When it comes to any kind of infidelity, my husband has never given me any reason to doubt his loyalty, morality, or decency. And I am forever grateful for that. This had to do with a decision Michael made that negatively affected both of us, but he never consulted me or even told me about it until the consequences began affecting me as well.

I didn't find out what had happened from Michael. I found out as the consequences of his decision started coming down on me, and I was angry. When I confronted him about it, he knew he had done the wrong thing, and he apologized. That helped, but the damage had been done, and I would still be the one to suffer the most because of it. Even though he had sincerely apologized and I eventually said I forgave him, I couldn't let it go. The situation still kept coming up in my mind and affecting my attitude. My heart was broken, and I felt betrayed.

I went to God about it right away, of course, because I knew that if I didn't get rid of the unforgiveness in my heart, it would bring even greater consequences for me than my husband's decision had. Every week I asked my prayer group to pray with me about my unforgiveness, and each time I would seem to be better—at least for a while. But the anger and pain would come back to me again in full force every time I was faced with the consequences of the decision—a decision I myself would never have dreamed of making.

LIVING WITH DOUBT AND HOPELESSNESS

The whole situation began eating at me so much that it affected my attitude toward life and the future. It was as if I couldn't look forward to anything anymore. Without a doubt, my hurting and hard heart affected my relationship with my husband. I prayed for a God-please-get-us-out-of-this-mess kind of miracle, but because I couldn't see any way out of it myself, I doubted God would do anything—or that He even wanted to. Why would He? Does God redeem our stupid mistakes every time we make them? Doesn't He sometimes—or often—let us suffer the consequences of our decisions so we learn to seek Him first and be led by Him when we make decisions?

There's something about being older in years that makes certain consequences of bad judgment more unbearable.

Hopelessness set in and actually became a part of me. From the day I found out about the bad decision and began reaping the consequences, things changed. There's something about being older in years that makes certain consequences of bad judgment more unbearable. You don't feel you have the strength to endure them or make up for them anymore. When you are young and have most of your life ahead of you, it is easier to be positive about mistakes and misfortune. After all, you've got time to correct them and get beyond them. Bad decisions and their consequences are not nearly as overwhelming then.

For months I prayed and prayed—every day, many times a day—that God would take my unforgiveness and bitterness away, but the breakthrough I needed and desired didn't come. I had let human solutions become more important in my mind than trust that God could get us through this. I let my God-given vision for the future be overtaken by my human fear of what could happen.

CONFESSION AND CHANGE

Finally, one morning as I was again reading the Bible and praying about this matter, God spoke to my heart as clearly as I have ever heard Him speak to me. I knew it was God because what He clearly impressed upon my heart was definitely not something I would have come up with on my own. And it certainly was not a lie of the enemy. I felt that unmistakable renewing and refreshing rain washing over the severely parched areas of my soul. It was God, and I knew it.

I was lifting this situation up to God once again and saying for the hundredth time, "Lord, I confess my unforgiveness. Please take it away. Take away the bad attitude I have toward my husband." That's when I heard God speak clearly to my heart: "Your attitude is a choice you make."

God didn't elaborate, and He didn't have to. It was clear to me. I knew in that instant that nothing would change—neither in me or in my situation—unless I chose to adopt the attitude God wanted me to have. And I knew what that attitude should be.

I had memorized the fruit of the Spirit, but I looked up that passage anyway. I needed to see with my own eyes so as to implant firmly on my brain the exact virtues I needed to have. I needed to choose to have an attitude of love, joy, peace, patience, kindness, goodness, faithfulness, gentleness, and self-control. These are the natural result of the Holy Spirit living in us, but they are produced only when we choose to allow the Holy Spirit to fully control our personalities. He doesn't force us to bear fruit; we invite Him to do so. We shut down production any time we choose our way over His way. And we can think we have a handle on this until something bad happens and we become the victim of someone else's bad choice. Without proper feeding and tending, fruit withers and dies.

UNFORGIVENESS WILL BE REVEALED

The Bible says that we must have faith, hope, and love—and love is most important because it lasts forever. I needed to choose to have *faith* that God could work in this situation—even though I could not fathom how. And I needed to put my *hope* entirely in Him—not in myself, not in my husband, not in other people. Most of all, I needed to have *love*. But love is suffocated by unforgiveness, and unforgiveness reveals itself even when we try to tell ourselves that we are completely free of it. Unforgiveness refuses to be hidden.

I needed to choose to have faith that
God could work in this situation—even
though I could not fathom how.

Immediately upon hearing God's message to me, I was faced with the choice I needed to make about my attitude. I saw how unforgiveness had affected my relationship with my husband and even joy around others. It disgusted me that I had been making the wrong choice every day. Who's bad decision was greater—my husband's or mine?

Of course I knew all this in my head, but apparently I didn't really know it in my heart until something bad happened. I fully repented. I knew from then on, I had to make a choice every day—perhaps even every hour—about my attitude.

Every time I knew I was going to see my husband—especially first thing in the morning—I made the choice to greet him with the love, joy, and peace of God in my heart. I was going to have an attitude that says, "God reigns in my life and His Spirit lives in me, and I give control of my heart to the Holy Spirit." I decided that whatever I said to my husband would be positive and uplifting. I would choose my attitude. And it would no longer be irritation.

From the moment I started doing that, the biggest miracle of all happened: I began to trust that God could do a miracle in our situation. It was not that I didn't think He could do a miracle—I know that God can do the impossible—it was that I didn't know if He would want to.

MAKING THE RIGHT CHOICE

I finally forgave my husband completely, and the issue between us stopped coming up in my mind all the time. Our relationship improved right away. I haven't seen a miracle yet with regard to this problem, but I have seen a slight lessening of the impact of the consequences, which came from a place I would never have expected. This is a miracle in itself, I believe, and I rejoice in it.

I am not perfect in this attitude thing, and there are some days I forget to make that choice. But I am able to catch myself and then get on board with God's direction. I am thoroughly convinced that the choice of attitude is mine, and I try—more times than not—to make the right one.

Stormie Omartian is the best-selling author of The Power of a Praying . . . *series. In addition, she and her husband, Michael, have written hundreds of songs. The Omartians have been married for more than thirty-five years and have three grown children. You can visit her website at www.stormieomartian.com.*

15

Deliberately Seek the Lord

Phil and Heather Joel

The best marriage advice I've ever received didn't come from the lips of an old sage or from the pages of a book filled with marital wisdom. Instead it came through my daughter, my firstborn—and she didn't even know how to speak at the time.

It was the fall of 2000, and Heather and I had been married nearly six years. We were thoroughly enjoying married life together. I'd been in the United States for seven years, and at that time was a member of the Christian band *Newsboys*. I had also signed a record deal and released my first solo CD.

Heather also had her own thing going on. She was the onscreen host of a TV show on CMT (Country Music Television) called *Hit Trip*. She would take trips to cities all around the States with the big country music stars and a film crew and do all the fun things that each city had to offer. It's pretty fun to be able to finish up a concert and go back to the tour bus or hotel and watch your wife on TV.

LIVING THE AMERICAN DREAM

Our work and travel schedules were very busy, and life was moving at a pretty quick pace. But as far as we knew, our lives were everything they were meant to be. There we were—in our late twenties—living the lives we'd always dreamed of. We had each other, fun careers, and all the stuff that culture tells us we're supposed to have. We were living the American Dream. We even had a white picket fence around our house! The only thing missing from our American Dream was the pitter-patter of tiny feet, but in October 2000 that void was filled by the arrival of Phynley, our daughter.

I was so concerned with getting the car seat secure in the backseat and making sure the house was baby safe and all that kind of stuff that the reality of my "fatherhood" didn't hit me until late one night when I was sitting out under the stars on the back porch. It was there that it hit me: *Wham!* "You're a dad! You have a daughter and that makes you a dad!" I'm sure this sounds lame to most people, but I guess I'd been running on some kind of newbie parent adrenaline that had kept me from catching up with what had happened. It really hadn't dawned on me until that moment.

That was a *huge* moment for me, but even larger were the questions that followed, questions that needed my honest answers: "What kind of a man is my daughter going to see in me? What kind of man am I *really?*"

SOMETHING STIRRING

When I shared my "back porch experience" with Heather, she seemed to understand to a certain degree what I was feeling. It was an especially sobering time. We both had a sense that God was stirring up something inside each of us.

After a few weeks of sensing this quiet stirring, we found ourselves in an emergency situation. I won't go into the details, but we needed to pray, *really* pray *big*-time and truly cry out to God. The type of prayer that we were used to offering before meals or bed wasn't gonna cut it. This needed *real-deal* prayer, the kind that only people who really know God can pray. Heather and I didn't know what to do, what to say, or what to pray. We realized in that moment that we weren't able to call out to God because we didn't really know the God to whom we were trying to call out.

Heather and I were both lifelong church kids. We both grew up in Christian homes with Christian parents. But we realized that even though we knew a lot *about* God, we didn't truly *know Him.*

We realized that even though we knew a lot
about *God, we didn't truly* know Him.

God was showing us our true condition. We were beginning to see that the form of Christianity we were living out was not what He desired for us. We sensed there was more, and we wanted it. We felt that the Lord was reaching out to us and that we needed to reach back. He'd gotten our attention, and our hearts, ears, and eyes were open to Him in a new way. But we weren't exactly sure what to do next.

We both loved the Lord and had a true desire to know Him. We authentically desired to become the people He created us to be. We just didn't have a plan. And without a plan for pursuing a real relationship with God, we'd ended up in a cycle of neutrality.

A SIMPLE PLAN

We decided that if God could really, truly be known, we were going after Him. And we came up with a simple little plan. We determined to wake up early—before the phones started ringing, before the baby started crying, in the quiet of the morning. We knew it was the best time both of us could carve out of our schedule so we could tackle this plan together. We decided to use a one-year Bible reading schedule that had the month and day listed with the portions of Scripture we were to read for that day. Like I said, it was simple.

And so we began—Heather in the living room, me in the dining room. I remember opening my Bible and first simply asking, "Lord, here I am. Meet with me, please?"

The next morning we did the same thing, and the next morning. Again and again we'd show up, desiring to meet with God and hear from Him. Some days it was tougher than others; some days it was nearly impossible. I mean, for one thing it's a well-known fact that musicians don't do well early in the morning—seriously! Anyway, after we had done this every morning for around three months, something really cool happened. Midway into our time one morning, the two of us met at the coffee machine for a second cup. Heather looked at me and said, "Phil, it's *working!*" She was so excited! The funny thing was, I knew exactly what she meant because I felt it too. "I know," I said. "It *is* working!"

What had slowly started happening without our even realizing it was this: day after day for three months we'd been spending time with the Lord, consistent time, reading the Word and praying. We were feeding on truth and beginning to get to know the Lord. We were growing in a real-deal *relationship* with Him, and we were beginning to learn the sound of His voice. From that moment on the Bible became our lifeline, and as we continued to press in to it, we could feel the Lord speaking to us and showing us things about Himself that we'd never seen before!

We were feeding on truth and
beginning to get to know the Lord.

Things began to jump off the pages. We'd both been journaling during those months, and now we almost couldn't stop writing—the Lord was showing us so much—about Himself, about us, about our marriage, about parenting, about our careers. This *relationship* was beginning to change us—and it still is changing us.

PRAYER CHANGES EVERYTHING

In the midst of this transformation, we recognized that this was the *real* beginning of our marriage adventure together. We'd never felt such excitement about our lives or such peace. As close as Heather and I had been before, it didn't compare to the closeness we were experiencing as we traveled this journey together. We began to understand—and we're still finding out about—the incredible oneness of marriage. What a brilliant design!

That initial experience and the discovery of God's desire and availability for real relationship with Himself happened over ten years ago, and I have to say that deliberately seeking the Lord every day is far and away the *best* marriage advice I have ever received! It has changed literally everything about our marriage and our lives. We start out every day on the same page.

Do we still have tough times?

Yes.

Do we have a perfect marriage?

No.

But here's the deal: Our desire is to hear from the Lord as we consistently put ourselves in a position to have Him show us and teach us things we'd never know on our own. So when the tough times come (as they will continue to do) and when the challenges enter in, we're walking them out with the Lord. We have a totally different perspective from what we had at the beginning of our marriage.

Our desire is to hear from the Lord as we consistently put ourselves in a position to have Him show us and teach us things we'd never know on our own.

Heather and I are hooked . . . *hooked* on the Lord. We're hooked on knowing Him and hearing from Him during time we spend alone with Him in the Word and prayer. Our time with Him is not some check-it-off-the-list religious activity, but a meeting with the true and living God who loves speaking truth to us and having us walk with Him and enjoy Him.

This relationship with God is the key that makes all other relationships take their rightful place and fulfill their rightful purpose in my life. I believe that as the man goes, so goes the marriage. My wife depends on my walking with God on a daily basis. She knows I'm going to do my best to hear from Him and to walk in a way that pleases Him and serves her and our family.

So let me finish by saying, "Thanks, Phyn. Thanks for being born into our family and for somehow advising me to take stock of my life and my relationship with Jesus. Thanks for stirring up a renewed desire to know God and to pursue

Him with fervent passion as if my life, my marriage, and my family depend on it—because they do."

You have changed the way I do everything
You have changed the way I wear my wedding ring
You have changed the way I treat my family
You have changed the way I see all my friends
You have changed the ways that I spend my time
You've changed the ways that I use my mind
You have changed the things that I spend money on
You have changed everything I ever thought was mine
You have changed my emotions, You have steadied me
You've changed my eyes and what I let them see
You've changed the course of my history
Thank God You're STILL changing me![1]

1. Lyric excerpted from "Changed" on *The deliberatePeople Album* by Phil Joel. Used by permission.

Phil Joel was a bass player and vocalist with the Newsboys for thirteen years. He has made six solo albums. In 2004, Phil and Heather began deliberatePeople—a ministry focused on communicating God's desire for us to live in true relationship first with Him and then with those around us. Phil and Heather have two children and make their home near Nashville.

16

Believe Your Spouse Wants Your Best

Jeff and Shaunti Feldhahn

We can still remember the exact moment that our marriage began the fundamental change from average to something we enjoy every single day. It was when we finally realized what Shaunti's parents meant when, at our wedding, they offered this advice: "You have to believe that the other person has your best in mind." Shaunti is going to take you back to that moment in time . . .

SHAUNTI'S STORY

Jeff and I were standing in the kitchen of our New York City apartment. We had been married about three years, and for all of that time our biggest source of conflict was how much time Jeff put in at the office. As in, so much time that I rarely saw him. We were a few years out of graduate school at

Harvard (him in law, me in public policy), and we both had fast-paced jobs. But Jeff's job was insane. He was a junior associate at a sweatshop law firm where eighty-hour weeks were the norm. He scrambled to keep up with the load his partners required. On an average day, he would leave our apartment at 7AM and return at 11PM. He usually had to work many hours on weekends, and he would often go in ultra-early on Saturdays so he'd be done by midday, and we could have a few precious hours together.

I soon learned that this barbaric schedule is the norm for big-city lawyers who simply have no life. All the normal things that newlyweds do—hang out with friends, go on vacations, go together to church and small group—were difficult for us to plan. Often, I would end up going alone.

I have to admit, I didn't handle it well. It seemed as if our newlywed years were being sacrificed on the altar of his job. I was furious with his partners for working him so hard and seeming so unconcerned about things like canceling our vacation at the last minute because some deal came up. And truth be told, I was often angry with Jeff too. He was working hard and was exhausted all the time, but I felt like he could change the situation if he really wanted to. The fact that he didn't change it made me feel like he cared about work more than me.

As we stood in the kitchen that night, the usual conflict flared up as he broke the news that one of the partners had just assigned him to a deal that would require working around the clock that weekend. It also meant cancelling plans to get out of the city with friends.

"Can't you just tell them no?" I pleaded with Jeff for what seemed like the hundredth time that year.

He shook his head as he unloaded the dishwasher. "I'm sorry." It was past midnight, and he looked wearier than anyone in his midthirties should look. "It's a $4 billion deal, and they need me to handle most of the gruntwork with some other junior attorneys."

As I saw yet another set of plans crumbling before me, tears started running down my cheeks. I had been looking forward to being with our friends and finally having a chance to relax. I didn't know how to handle the intense feelings of disappointment. And I didn't know how to handle the feeling that I was a low priority to my husband.

"Please don't cry," he said, and his normally even-keeled demeanor cracked a bit. "I don't have any choice!"

"Of course you have a choice!" My tears were coming in earnest now. "They are trying to work you into an early grave, and you won't do anything to stop them. You never just put your foot down and tell them no. It makes me feel like you don't care about me!"

As he shoved a drinking glass onto the shelf and swung toward me, I was astonished to see tears springing to his eyes. "Do you think I *want* to be working this much? I'm doing this *because* I care about you!"

Feelings began pouring out of Jeff that he had not known how to articulate before. "Do you think I like being exhausted all the time, and having no time with you, and missing our small group, and having no time for myself? But we have $135,000 in student loan debt and a nice apartment in Manhattan, and I have no choice. I need to figure out how to provide for us, and this is the only way I know how to do it! I don't like this any more than you do, but I'm doing it because I love you!"

I was overwhelmed. Suddenly, for the first time, I truly got it. Among the many other things I saw in that moment, I understood that his motivation toward me honestly was good rather than selfish or uncaring. And what began to change our relationship from that moment on wasn't just that I started to truly grasp the deep things in his heart about self-doubt, a longing for my respect, and the burden to provide—an understanding that eventually culminated in my researching and writing *For Women Only: What You Need to Know About the Inner Lives of Men.* No, for us, the most important transformation came as I realized that for years, whenever we had difficulties, I had actually been assuming the worst of Jeff (he is choosing work over me) instead of the best (he hates being away from me, but feels as if he has no choice).

On his side, Jeff had a similar realization. And once our eyes were opened to this and we began to try to believe the best of each other, everything about our marriage changed.

Once we began to try to believe the best of each other, everything about our marriage changed.

MAKING THE FUNDAMENTAL SWITCH

We eventually moved away from New York in search of a healthier pace of life, and within a few years we unexpectedly found ourselves researching and writing multiple relationship books, including *For Women Only* and *For Men Only*. We have been amazed to see how God has used them to open the eyes of men and women to some life-changing truths that they didn't know about the opposite sex.

But above all the other truths stands one that applies to the vast majority of marriages. And that truth is the one our parents told us about at our wedding, now seventeen years ago: no matter what it feels like at that moment, your spouse cares about you and wants your best.

BELIEVING THE BEST ABOUT YOUR SPOUSE

In our research, Jeff and I have found that believing that one thing—that your spouse wants the best for you even in the face of seemingly contrary evidence—not only solves so many problems, but also prevents problems to begin with.

So what does it look like to believe the best about your spouse? Here are four relatively small actions that make a huge difference:

1. Identify the sneaky negatives.
The next time you are having a hard time with your spouse—he's hurt your feelings, or she's done that thing again that

she promised she'd stop doing—take a two-minute time-out and ask yourself this question: What am I assuming about my spouse's motivation? Often you will realize it is quite a negative assumption: *He knew how that would make me feel—and he said it anyway.* Or *She knows how much I dislike that. She just doesn't care how much this matters to me.*

2. Replace them with the positives.

Even in difficult times and during emotional arguments, those negative assumptions simply aren't true for the vast majority of spouses (nine in ten according to our surveys so far). So, next, ask yourself this question: What could be another, more generous explanation of why my spouse did that? Then take captive the negative belief about your spouse's motivation. Simply decide to assume that the positive one is true: *He just didn't realize how much that would hurt.* Or *She does know how much I dislike that—but it's hard for her to stop, and I know she's trying.*

3. Act on the new belief.

Your new awareness won't help you unless you act on it. If it is indeed true that, for example, he just didn't realize how much his words would hurt you, then it would be destructive and wrong for you to lash out at him for being an insensitive lout. Instead, after your two-minute break, you could say, "I know you didn't mean it, but when you said that, it really hurt my feelings. Let me explain why." The amazing thing about acting on these new assumptions is that pretty soon you don't have to force it. You simply don't have the negative assumptions to begin with.

4. *Learn the truth about your spouse.*

Just as our spouses do hurtful things to us without realizing it or intending to hurt us, we do hurtful things to them. Usually, it's because we simply don't understand the other person's innermost needs and fears. We make such an effort to care for our spouses, but we don't realize we are trying hard in the wrong areas. And we don't realize, for instance, that we are causing our spouse to feel ignored, hurt, or unhappy. For example, a wife can say, "I love you" and do many loving things, but never realize that because a man's greatest need is respect, her husband is depressed because he never hears her say things like "You did such a great job on that presentation," or "Thank you for mowing the lawn when it was so hot outside." (Or if she does offer such respectful thanks, she unknowingly cancels it out by adding, "But you missed a spot.")

LET UNDERSTANDING TRANSFORM YOUR MARRIAGE

All those years ago, Jeff was working under the assumption that what I most needed was security, which meant (he thought) living in a nice doorman building in Manhattan, paying off our student loans, and putting away money for retirement—all of which were paid for by the high salary that went with his insane job. And he felt confused and stressed over what he felt were my impossible expectations that he should be able to do all of this *and* be available a lot more, since in his position that simply wasn't possible.

Once we had that breakthrough, just as I realized his choices truly reflected a deep love rather than a lack of it, he realized that I really didn't care about "the stuff" more than I cared about him. He realized I honestly was willing to trade the high salary and the glamorous Manhattan life to get more of him.

The ultimate decision to make our marriage a priority by moving away from Manhattan was a pretty big deal. But in the end it is just one example of the fundamental day-to-day transformation that happens in our marriage when we decided to believe the best of each other—just as my parents had advised us to do all those years ago.

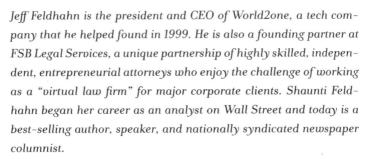

Jeff Feldhahn is the president and CEO of World2one, a tech company that he helped found in 1999. He is also a founding partner at FSB Legal Services, a unique partnership of highly skilled, independent, entrepreneurial attorneys who enjoy the challenge of working as a "virtual law firm" for major corporate clients. Shaunti Feldhahn began her career as an analyst on Wall Street and today is a best-selling author, speaker, and nationally syndicated newspaper columnist.

Jeff and Shaunti are active leaders in their church. They make their home in Atlanta with their two children.

17

The Power of Taking a Time-Out

Michael and Amy Smalley

Before Michael and I (Amy) first got married, I read all of the Gary Smalley books I could find. The one thing that sticks out to me as the greatest advice I received in marriage was this single word: *honor.* When times got truly tough, I was drawn to this word like a beacon in the night. I wanted to honor God and Michael. I often got irritated when I was looking at our personality differences with dishonor in my heart. When we learned how to slow down and take a time-out, we were better able to honor each other's strengths and growth areas.

New York City is our favorite place on earth. We love the lights, the people, the energy, the food, the culture, and the fact that you typically get to share a table at a restaurant with a complete stranger because there's simply not enough space for the masses of people who all want to eat at the same place. As Johnny Carson is reported to have said, "New York is an exciting town where something is happening all the time, most of it unsolved." There's just no other place on earth quite like New York City, and we've been traveling there for many years to vacation and minister. So you would think that the first time we took our kids to experience the wonder and pure awesomeness of New York, we would be on our best behavior trying to make the trip perfect. Well, life—and marriage specifically—can sure get messed up, and messed up quickly.

We'd been in New York for less than forty-eight hours when we found ourselves working our way toward the Staten Island Ferry in Lower Manhattan. If you've traveled extensively to NYC, you know that the best (and cheapest) way to see the Statue of Liberty is to take the *free* Staten Island Ferry. Our three kids wanted to see the statue, and Mommy and Daddy did not want to pay the exorbitant prices to take the official tour, so we pumped up how incredible it is to ride the Staten Island Ferry. Off we went to board the train to the South Ferry stop. Little did we know when we boarded the train that, in roughly twenty minutes, we'd be fiercely engaged in one of those fights that springs up from nowhere and takes you on a ridiculous roller-coaster ride of emotions.

RIDING THE ROLLER COASTER

As we ushered our family off the train and began walking toward the ferry, Amy excitedly announced to me, "Oh, hey! I totally forgot to tell you that I actually connected with Brady earlier today because he saw your Facebook updates about being in New York City." Brady was one of her closest friends from Baylor University and her yell-leading partner for a season of football. We had not really connected with Brady for many years, and she told me he happened to be in NYC working on a big project for his company. "So I told him that we'd meet up tonight for dinner so he could meet our kids!"

Amy's eyes were filled with the excitement and anticipation of showing off her kids to one of her closest college friends. Any normal husband might share this excitement with his wife, but not me! Oh no! I had much better plans, and I totally flipped out.

Honestly, I had no clue why I escalated so fast. I lost my mind in a matter of seconds and actually found myself saying—and I'm actually quoting here—"What kind of a wife would make dinner plans on a family vacation without consulting with her husband?"

You are probably as surprised by my outburst of anger as I was at the time. Did my comment—my reaction—even make sense? It's as if I thought Amy was trying to destroy our family vacation by making spontaneous dinner plans with a close friend.

Amy looked at me in total confusion. She could not understand my anger, and, frankly, neither could I. But our confusion over my anger didn't stop me from going one step further—and I'm truly quoting myself . . . again—"You had no right to make plans without talking to me first, and if you make me go to this dinner, I promise, I will be rude the entire time!"

To this brilliant threat from a marriage and family expert who holds a master's degree in clinical psychology and is only a dissertation shy of a PhD in psychology, Amy responded, "Okay, then, how about we take a time-out and sit apart so we can cool off? If it's okay with you, let's just table this discussion until after the ferry ride. I'll make sure the kids get to see the Statue of Liberty." With that, I stomped off to the other side of the ferry and plopped down on a seat, alone and utterly confused about my actions.

REACTING VERSUS RESPONDING

Have you ever found yourself in a similar situation? No marriage is free of goofy, ridiculous arguments that seem to spring up from out of the blue. The issue is not about eliminating these kinds of interactions; unfortunately, we live in a broken, fallen world full of sinful, mistake-prone people. The apostle Paul himself knew the struggle: "I see another law at work in the members of my body, waging war against the law of my mind and making me a prisoner of the law of sin at work within my members" (Romans 7:23). We will always battle against our sinful nature, but we can learn how to start *responding* instead of *reacting*.

Michael *reacted* to my (Amy) rather innocent dinner plans instead of *responding*. We want to make a clear distinction between reacting and responding. Reacting is when someone immediately lashes out or shuts down because their feelings have been hurt or they discover something they do not like. It is our natural "enslaved to sin" reaction. Responding, on the other hand, is when we stop and think before we speak or act. When we respond to a situation, we have actually put some thought into what we are about to say or do. Responding is taking our sin nature by the throat and telling it to get out of the way.

If you want to start responding instead of reacting to a conflict in your relationship, James 1:19–20 offers this guideline: "Everyone should be quick to listen, slow to speak and slow to become angry, for man's anger does not bring about the righteous life that God desires." The absolute best thing a couple can do when conflict erupts is to stop whatever they are doing and take a time-out.

TIME-OUT: NOT JUST FOR KIDS

The first major rule of a time-out is to call one the moment you get upset. Simply say, "I'm upset and I need a break before I can talk about this. Can we talk in an hour?" Now you may be thinking, "Isn't a time-out just a way to avoid the issue?" No. Avoidance is when you simply walk away from the discussion never to talk about it again. A time-out is different because you have to set a time-in. It is not a time-out unless you have a time-in. Before you walk *away* from each other, you'd better know the exact time you are going to walk back *to* each other.

The first major rule of a time-out is to
call one the moment you get upset.

You protect yourselves when you stop arguments by walking away before they get crazy. The following list offers specific ways a time-out can keep the relationship free from nasty fights:

1. As mentioned above, the first thing to do is let your spouse know that you need a time-out. You might say something like "I need a break," "I'm about to say something I don't mean," or "I don't feel like this conversation is heading in a good direction."

2. Then negotiate a time to come back together and talk. "I think I can talk in about two hours. Is that okay with you?" Or "Can we talk about this tomorrow after I've gotten some sleep?" Or "Can I just have thirty minutes to calm down and think?" Settle on a time that works for both of you.

3. Take the break and leave each other alone.

4. Pray, pray, and pray some more.

The power of the Holy Spirit is at the heart of any great marriage. Jesus not only died as payment for our sins, but He also died so that the Holy Spirit would come (John 16:7). One of the blessings of the Holy Spirit's presence in us and with us is that He will convict and guide us throughout our lives when we tap in to His power. When you pray during your time-out, you allow yourself to be influenced by the Holy Spirit.

LISTENING TO THE HOLY SPIRIT

Now, coming back to our fight in NYC, I (Michael) had sat down alone on the opposite side of the ferry from my family. I was angry and I was confused. I honestly had no idea why I'd reacted so terribly to Amy's dinner plans. Before I let too much time pass, I began to cry out to God. My prayer went something like "God, I literally have no idea why I'm so angry at Amy for making these dinner plans. Help me understand."

I sat in the chair for a long moment, quietly trying to listen to what God had to say to me about what was really going on within me. Then, like a bolt of lightning, the Holy Spirit did what the Holy Spirit promises to do. If not for the power of the Holy Spirit, I can assure you that I would never had understood why I was so upset.

As usual, my overreaction had absolutely nothing to do with Amy or the dinner plans; instead, it had everything to do with me and my own junk. The Holy Spirit tenderly helped me see the real reason I was so upset. I was afraid of what our friend would think of my weight gain. I do not like to be this vulnerable, but I'm doing it because you need to know that when you really lose control and handle yourself poorly, 99 percent of the time you are doing so because of your own junk. In this case, I was afraid that our friend would take one look at me and think, "Daaang!" I actually thought he would say something out loud that would hurt and humiliate me in front of my kids.

When you really lose control and handle yourself poorly, 99 percent of the time you are doing so because of your own junk.

When I realized what I was really upset about, my heart calmed down, and I was ready to approach Amy as we disembarked the ferry. I lightly touched her hand and asked if she'd be willing to let me apologize for my attitude. She willingly turned around and waited for my apology. I looked at her and shared what the Holy Spirit had revealed to me on the ferry. Of course she felt sad for me and my own issues about my weight. I said to her, "Obviously I am not going to make you cancel the dinner plans for tonight, and I am definitely not going to show up and be rude the entire time. I can't even believe I said that. I apologize for overreacting, Amy, and I'm willing to go out tonight and have fun with you, the kids, and Brady."

DEVELOPING A GAME PLAN

Michael never would have gotten to this point without taking the time-out and running to God in prayer. Too many vacations and date nights are ruined because couples do not take a time-out, think, and pray. We ended up developing a game plan for what we would do just in case Brady did get hurtful. I (Amy) wasn't too concerned about that happening, but it was great for the two of us to process together how we would handle the situation if it did arise. We were a team again because we took the time to allow ourselves to calm down and honor God in our conversations.

We did go to dinner that evening with Brady, and to Michael's joy, Brady never mentioned anything about his weight gain, nor did he try to humiliate Michael in front of the kids! We had a great time with an old friend.

Next time you're in a similar situation, try a time-out, pray, and see if you don't gain a clearer understanding of your true feelings and find yourself able to respond rather than react. That time-out just may be what you and your marriage need.

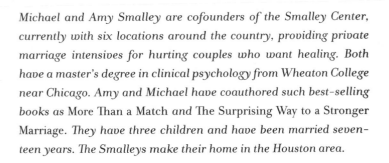

Michael and Amy Smalley are cofounders of the Smalley Center, currently with six locations around the country, providing private marriage intensives for hurting couples who want healing. Both have a master's degree in clinical psychology from Wheaton College near Chicago. Amy and Michael have coauthored such best-selling books as More Than a Match *and* The Surprising Way to a Stronger Marriage. *They have three children and have been married seventeen years. The Smalleys make their home in the Houston area.*

18

The Convicting Question That's Changing Our Marriage

Lee Strobel

If you open the spiral-bound calendar I keep on my desk, you'll notice something odd in the box marking the first day of every month. Each box has a set of letters followed by a question mark: HWILTBMTM?

That's what I do to remind myself a dozen times a year to take to heart the best advice I've received on marriage. It came in the form of a question that marriage experts Les and Leslie Parrott urge spouses to ask themselves: "How would I like to be married to me?"

Wow! *That's* a convicting question! I winced when I first read it. And over time it has prompted me to reexamine my behavior and attitudes, my priorities and actions, my decisions and manners. To keep this issue on the forefront of my mind, I force myself to look at those initials so that every month I make a fresh commitment to becoming a better spouse.

Even after forty years of marriage, Leslie and I are still working to strengthen our relationship. We're well aware that we started out on a shaky foundation. We were young and immature when we wed. Neither of us was following Christ at the time—in fact, I was an atheist—and we didn't agree on a common morality or how to raise the kids. We didn't understand ourselves, much less each other. And I selfishly elevated my journalism career above our relationship.

Given this formula for disaster, why didn't our marriage self-destruct? I'll give you one word that I am absolutely convinced is the reason why: *God.*

If you ask why we have been able to build a strong marriage on an initially unstable foundation, I'd say this: the degree to which we've flourished as a couple is the degree to which we've cooperated with God and let Him change us as individuals into new creations in Christ (2 Corinthians 5:17).

A NEW CREATION

It's no surprise that the areas in which God helps us grow and change contribute to a successful marriage. Consider how He moves us down a series of continuums—from being self-centered toward being more servant-oriented, from being judgmental toward being more accepting, from having a retaliatory attitude toward being more forgiving, from being defensive toward being more willing to admit our faults.

"Willpower does not change men," wrote Henry Drummond. "Time does not change men. Christ does."[1] And ever since we received Jesus Christ as our Lord and Savior, He has not allowed Leslie or me to remain static. Instead, He has gently been transforming our attitudes, values, character, and priorities over time.

How would I like to be married to me? If I were still the profane Lee, the drunken Lee, the chronically angry Lee, the blatantly immoral Lee, and the self-destructive Lee that I was early in our marriage, I honestly don't see how Leslie could have stayed with me for the long haul. While I don't want to pretend I'm further down the road of transformation than I am, with the help of God I'm at least making progress on the journey!

How would I like to be married to me?

Reflecting on our marriage, I can see three key areas where God has helped Leslie and me grow. The first involves communication. Over time, God has been moving us from being faultfinders toward being mutual encouragers.

BECOME AN ENCOURAGER

We all come into marriage with expectations—and invariably our spouse falls short. Our natural response is to try to "fix" them, and the easiest way to do that is to point out their shortcomings and instruct them on how they should change—*right?*

Well, not exactly. Actually, this is the faultfinding trap. Why don't you do this or that? Why aren't you more like him or her? Why can't you be more outgoing, or treat my parents better, or spend less time at the office? You always do this; you never do that.

As H. Norman Wright points out, faultfinding deeply wounds our spouse. In effect, we're saying, "I don't accept you for who you are. You don't measure up and I can't accept you until you do. You're not good enough for me."[2] Those are devastating messages! And our natural impulse when someone points out our faults is to turn around and point out theirs. Suddenly, we're caught in a downward relational spiral.

Leslie and I found sage advice in Matthew 7:1: "Do not judge and criticize and condemn others, so that you may not be judged and criticized and condemned yourselves" (AMP).

That's why, more and more, Leslie and I are becoming each other's biggest cheerleaders. We praise the best qualities in each other. We try to accept each other unconditionally. We paint a vision of what God can do with each other if we stay true to Him. Yes, there are times when we need to deal with our faults, but now there's such a deep reservoir of goodwill that we're able to hear critical words without as much defensiveness as we had in the past.

CELEBRATE UNIQUENESS

Our second area of growth has focused on our compatibility. Here, God has been moving Leslie and me from clashing over our differences toward celebrating our uniqueness.

And do we have differences! Leslie's a feeler; I'm a thinker. Leslie's a sensate who focuses on what she can see and touch; I'm an intuiter who plays with ideas and dreams of future possibilities. Leslie's a "just settle it" person; I'm a "play it by ear" type. Leslie's structured; I'm unstructured.

These contrasting personality traits used to cause all kinds of arguments between us. For a long time, Leslie thought I was intentionally being messy just to make her mad! She would pressure me to become more organized like she is, while I tried to get her to lighten up.

But over time God shaped our perspectives so we can appreciate our differences. We learned from Psalm 139:14 that we are each, in our own way, "fearfully and wonderfully made" by God. Leslie and I realized it's okay to be different from each other. We no longer feel like we need to badger each other into conforming to our own way of doing things. Instead, we try to validate each other's uniqueness and flex to accommodate each other.

Leslie, for instance, has given up trying to turn me into a structured person. She has come to understand that just because I don't organize my life into nice neat files like she does, doesn't mean I'm not organized in my own way. And in light of her being so organized, I've learned to be punctual. I try not to mess up her space. When I'm dealing with a matter that I know is important to her, I try not to procrastinate. We've found that validating each other—instead of picking each other apart—has been a major contributor to the longevity of our relationship.

FACE YOUR CONFLICTS

The third area where we've been growing deals with conflict resolution. Over the years, God has been moving us from being conflict-avoiders toward becoming conflict-facers.

We learned from Proverbs 27:17 that we should sharpen one other as "iron sharpens iron." This imagery suggests conflict—*even sparks!*—and we've discovered that lovingly working through conflict sharpens us as people and as a couple.

Like a lot of spouses, Leslie and I avoided conflict for much of our marriage. But our unresolved hurts drove a wedge between us. Now we've learned to follow what we call the "stop, look, and listen" approach. First, when conflict arises, we *stop* being defensive and honestly consider whether there's a seed of truth in what the other person is saying.

Second, we prayerfully *look* for mutually acceptable solutions that will not only resolve this immediate quarrel but which might help us deal with this entire category of conflict. In other words, we try to look beyond the argument at hand and see how this disagreement might fit into a broader pattern of conflict that we need to deal with on a deeper level.

Third, we *listen*. James 1:19 says, "Everyone should be quick to listen, slow to speak and slow to become angry." The key is to listen with what psychologists call "the third ear." This means becoming attentive to the emotions beneath our words.

Sometimes we'll argue over a minor matter, and Leslie will say, "I hear some hurt in your voice. I can tell you're upset by more than this little issue. What's really bothering you?" That opens the door to a deeper level of relating. Instead of skating on the surface of our conflict, we can dig down to the roots of our discontent and talk about the subterranean emotions that are fueling our behavior.

How would I like to be married to me? Ouch! When I'm confronted with that question twelve times a year, I still feel convicted. But forcing myself to ask it on a regular basis has been an application of some of the best advice I've ever received. It helps me do a gut-check: Am I a better husband this month than I was a year ago? Or five years ago? Am I communicating in an encouraging way? Am I celebrating Leslie's uniqueness? Am I facing conflict in a healthy manner by stopping, looking, and listening?

What about you? How would you like to be married to you? That might very well be a question that's worth putting down on your own calendar as you ask God to further shape you into the spouse that He wants you to be.

1. Henry Drummond, *The Greatest Thing in the World: Experience the Enduring Power of Love* (Grand Rapids, MI: Revell, 2011), 33.

2. H. Norman Wright, *Bringing Out the Best in Your Husband: Encourage Your Spouse and Experience the Relationship You've Always Wanted* (Ventura, CA: Regal, 2010), 40.

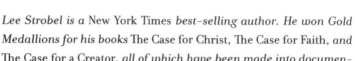

Lee Strobel is a New York Times *best-selling author. He won Gold Medallions for his books* The Case for Christ, The Case for Faith, *and* The Case for a Creator, *all of which have been made into documentaries distributed by Lionsgate. Lee and his wife, Leslie, have been married for forty years and live in Colorado. Their daughter, Allison, is a novelist, and their son, Kyle, holds two master's degrees from the Talbot School of Theology and a PhD in theology from the University of Aberdeen in Scotland. For more information about Lee and his book projects, visit www.LeeStrobel.com.*

WORTHY
PUBLISHING

IF YOU LIKED THIS BOOK . . .

- Tell your friends by going to: www.bestadviceievergoton marriage.com and clicking "LIKE"

- Log on to facebook.com/worthypublishing page, click "LIKE" and post a comment regarding what you enjoyed about the book

- Tweet "I recommend reading#bestadviceonmarriage by @FocusFamily @Worthypub"

- Hashtag: #MarriageAdvice

- Subscribe to our newsletter by going to www.worthy publishing.com

WORTHY PUBLISHING
FACEBOOK PAGE

WORTHY PUBLISHING
WEBSITE